"EGGS-A-COOK!"

The author acknowledges with thanks the loyal assistance of comrades who furnished him with useful information and confirmed much that was more or less hazy to him. Also his thanks are extended to those who came forward with the loan of the various photographs, official and otherwise, which are reproduced in the pages of this book.

DEDICATED TO COMRADES
STILL
"OVER THERE"

THE STORYTELLER.

"EGGS-A-COOK!"

THE STORY
OF THE
FORTY-FOURTH.

WAR—AS THE DIGGER SAW IT.

BY
CAPTAIN C. LONGMORE.

The Naval & Military Press Ltd

Published by
The Naval & Military Press Ltd
5 Riverside, Brambleside, Bellbrook
Industrial Estate, Uckfield, East Sussex,
TN22 1QQ England
Tel: +44 (0) 1825 749494
Fax: +44 (0) 1825 765701
www.naval-military-press.com
www.military-genealogy.com
www.militarymaproom.com

In reprinting in facsimile from the original, any imperfections are inevitably reproduced and the quality may fall short of modern type and cartographic standards.

INTRODUCTION.

In the absence of the publication to date of any histories of the older West Australian Battalions, it is with a certain amount of misgiving that I thrust that of the "infant" fighting Battalion of the West under the public eye. However, the 44th Battalion helped to make history, and during its short existence of three years, of which two years and three months were spent in Flanders, it certainly did not lower the fighting standard which the older A.I.F. Battalions had created.

In view of that fact alone, it is somebody's job to put on record the experiences of the Battalion. I possess no special qualifications as a writer, but as I was with the 44th from its inception until after its last stunt, with only two short periods away, I feel that I can make that job mine. That this story will chronicle completely the doings of the Battalion I do not claim, for the reason that I have written it from memory and have only checked times and places by reference to my own rather incomplete collection of field message books, and maps and orders issued in the field.

A few words are needed in explanation of the title "Eggs-a-Cook!" given to this story. That was the name bestowed on the Third Division when it first landed in England in July, 1916, by members of the other four Australian Divisions. The term originated in Egypt, where the natives sold hard-boiled eggs to the troops and shouted their wares as "Eggs-a-Cook!" It was applicable to the Third Division by

INTRODUCTION.

reason of the fact that their color patches were oval or egg-shaped. It implied that while the Third Division was training in England the "eggs were cooking" with the other four Australian Divisions—at that time engaged in the strenuous battles of the Somme—and that instead of being on Salisbury Plain, its place was "Over There." The nick-name whenever applied before the Division arrived in France generally provoked retaliation, and fistic arguments on Salisbury Plain were not uncommon. Once in France, however, the derision attached to the term commenced to die, and after the Battle of Messines, where the Third Division, fighting alongside the Fourth Australian Division, acquitted itself to the satisfaction of that already famous unit, the term "Eggs-a-Cook!" lost altogether its suggestion of inferiority. Towards the closing stages of the war in 1918, the Division was extraordinarily proud of its nick-name, feeling that by the part which it had played alongside its "big brothers" in the other Divisions, it had successfully turned a term of derision into one of approbation. For that reason, and because the 44th Battalion was a unit of the Third Division, I have named this story "Eggs-a-Cook!"

(Signed) C. LONGMORE, Capt.,

44th Battalion, A.I.F.

November 8, 1920.

CHAPTER I.

FORMATION.

The 44th Battalion was formed at Claremont, West Australia, in February, 1916. The commanding officer was Lieut.-Colonel W. O. Mansbridge, D.S.O., who had been originally an officer of the 16th Battalion, and who was invalided to Australia after service on Gallipoli, where for his services he had been awarded the D.S.O. The original company commanders were Major R. W. Everett, "A" Coy.; Capt. C. H. Lamb, "B" Coy.; Capt. W. H. Rockliffe, "C" Coy., and Capt. M. H. A'Beckett, "D" Coy. Of these Major Everett and Capt. Rockliffe had already seen service on Gallipoli with the 11th Battalion, and Capt. Lamb with the 28th Battalion. A few of the remaining officers were also invalided Gallipoli men, and among the rank and file were a sprinkling of men who were having a second go at the Hun.

The formation of the Battalion was not the easy task which it appeared to be on the surface. The one thousand souls comprising it were first of all divided into four companies. The men did not know anyone outside their own immediate cobbers; they did not know the sergeants or the officers; nor did they understand the meaning of the word discipline—that they had to be in camp at a certain hour each night, and that permission had to be obtained in order to leave camp.

The Cooks.

The new chum cooks were unused to cooking, at any rate according to rations. The first thing that everyone got up against was the "tucker." In the first place the cooks did not, at that time, display much of the initiative which afterwards made them famous. Everything seemed to go into the same pot, and, dished up, the result was called "stew." This stew was all right in its way, but it was too persistent. In addition to the stew there was bread and jam, and all ranks appreciated the open-handed manner in which the latter two items were issued. It ran to about one slice of bread and one spoonful of jam per man—but still, it was very nice, especially when it was in addition to the stew. Of course tea was issued also, and apart from the fact that there was always a shortage of something in its make-up, perhaps tea one day and sugar the next, it was always hot, and as it was warm weather then, the men appreciated that also, and did not forget to tell the cooks.

The poor cooks came in for a lot of abuse, and changes were frequent. The great appeal which the job had was that cooks! were exempt from parades. Naturally, the men who became finally the permanent company cooks were men of standing and character. Had they not been, they could not have held their responsible positions down for one week. As time went on they were appreciated at their true worth, and the cook-house and the cooks eventually provided the real "home touch" about the Battalion organisation.

Blues!

Khaki was not available for about two months after the Battalion was formed, and the soldiers' privilege of complaining was again well exercised. Blue uniforms were issued almost immediately on formation. They were a kind of dungaree with trouser buttons on the coats, no pockets in the trousers, and plenty of play around the ankles. With nice white

FORMATION.

hats and tan military boots with shining toe plates, heel plates and hobnails, the Battalion on parade looked well—from a distance. A surprising feature in those days was the lack of enthusiasm which the men detailed for picquet duty in Perth and Fremantle showed for the job when they had to go in "blues." They could not be persuaded that they looked like soldiers.

However, all these trifles were righted in time. Men got to know each other, their n.c.o.'s and officers; cooks learnt their jobs, khaki was issued, and one by one the matters of detail which make up the routine of a military camp became understood by all.

The Battalion can well be proud of its "toddling" days. The discipline and general bearing provided eloquent testimony to the commonsense of the men, and the judgment and tact of the commanding officer. The various "families" within the Battalion—officers, n.c.o.'s, and men—were very happy in their dealings between each other and within themselves. Looking back on the old days of formation it cannot be remembered that there was one really discordant note, and this in itself went a long way to contribute to the success which the Battalion ultimately gained.

CHAPTER II.

DRILL AND TRAINING.

Drill and training at Claremont was the same old grind familiar to all men of the A.I.F. Squad drill, physical jerks, rifle exercises, musketry, trench digging, machine guns, signalling, route marching, saluting and lectures from morning until night. How it was cursed! As he carried out each parade, the soldier wanted to know how the —— that particular item made him any more fit to fight the Hun. Why couldn't they send the Battalion overseas right away? What was the use of all this rot?

Faults.

From February to June it was hard going. In the earlier stages individual training was the rule. It is laid down in the big book that no military instructor is of any use whatever unless he can find and correct faults. Faults! They could find them anywhere, any time, and anyhow! On no occasion were any of the officers and n.c.o.'s at a loss for words. There was always some poor old private who did not have the correct slope, or his feet were not turned out properly, or else he was too slow, or even sometimes too quick. He did not get down smartly enough in the firing position, his heels stuck up, his eyes were not on the mark—and so on week in and week out.

The Battle of Buckland Hill.

A little more interesting from everyone's point of view was the field training. The Battalion then fought some big battles, which, owing to the strict censor-

Alick Maru and Dick Hilton, two "B" Company cooks who lasted right through the piece. The former was the Battalion "two-up" king.

THE "COOKHOUSE AND THE COOKS."

"OLD BILL."
Lieut.-Colonel W. O. Mansbridge, D.S.O., original
C.O. 44th Battalion, A.I.F.

ship prevailing over military operations at the time, failed to reach the newspapers. The Battle of Buckland Hill was a strenuous feat of arms. Will the machine-gunners forget their 600 yards run in short bursts, with covering fire, kerosene tins, ammunition, spare parts, water, and all the other odds and ends which, by reason of their superior status over the ordinary "pongo," the machine-gunners were graciously permitted to carry? Will "C" Coy. forget Lieut. Sammy Taylor's language when one "enemy" bomber threw a bomb (blue metal) which hit him (Sammy) on the head? And at the "pow-wow" after the operations the officers would be gathered around the colonel, who would listen to the various "furphies" put forward in explanation of the atrocious tactical blunders which were always committed on these field days, and who then would comment thereon and extinguish some budding Napoleons. Field work over, the Battalion always enjoyed the march home after a stunt. It was so good to finish a big battle ten miles away from camp, and towards evening march blithely back, with only a few small items in the shape of arms and equipment to carry—such as rifles, packs, water bottles, entrenching tools, etc. The most enjoyable thought the Diggers had then was that the officers had to march also, horses not being on the Battalion's ration state at the time.

The Battle of Stoney Ridge.

Another terrific battle fought during the training days was the Battle of Stoney Ridge. What wonderful bayonet charges were made there in the face of a terrific rattle from Bob Casey's kerosene tins! (Bob Casey was the machine-gun sergeant) It was during the course of this stunt that the defenders received that famous order "one round rapid—fire!"

Then the field firing at Osborne—hot, sandy, and prickly. In the rapid-firing practices the firer's rifle was always full of sand, and while he would be doing his best to work an obstinate bolt, a sergeant would roar at him to keep his heels down, and to take cover correctly, and not to move unnecessarily—and at the same time an officer would be describing the target by the clock and finger method, and by the time the bolt was got going, and the heels were down, and the cover was right, and the soldier was quiet and had found his target, it was time for the next rush forward—to repeat the whole process again. There's no doubt everyone enjoyed themselves, but not until they returned to camp and thought over the day's events with the aid of a pipe.

A band was formed only through the generosity of the citizens of Claremont. Although recognised as a necessity by them, the A.I.F. authorities did not provide for the issue of band instruments, but they graciously allowed about twenty odd men to be carried on the strength of Battalion headquarters, who could be utilised as bandsmen out of the line (if the public presented them with instruments), and in action they would act as stretcher-bearers. Anyhow, the citizens of Claremont presented the instruments, and the Battalion in a very short period had a band which could make itself heard, and which, later on in the piece, helped considerably to entertain the Diggers, at a time when any form of entertainment was of priceless value.

Church parades were attended by the troops almost to a man. They were not compulsory parades, but as it was either church parade or "fatigue," and the latter was for a longer period than the former, the church came in for more support among the military than it received from them in civilian life.

DRILL AND TRAINING. 17

The great social event of the Battalion's training days was the presentation of a flag to it by the citizens of Claremont. This was the occasion for an impressive ceremony on the show ground when Archbishop Riley consecrated the flag, and the Mayor of Claremont handed it over to the care of the Battalion—to have, to hold, and to keep flying through the stressful years to come.

During the month of May the stage was reached when Dame Rumor got busy. All hands had taken their final leave, and equipment and clothing down to the first field dressings and identity discs had been issued, and so, naturally, for six weeks before the actual embarkation some whisperer knew a chap who had the "dinkum oil" from the colonel's batman that they were off at daybreak in the morning, "but don't tell anyone as it's a secret." Of course everyone knows now how secrets were kept in the army! Some of these rumors were so persistent that they were believed and on these occasions practically the whole camp would rush off to say their last goodbyes, only to find next day that it was another "furphy," and that the programme for the day was the same old rifle exercises, form fours, etc. It was a long lane, but it had a turning however, and early in June, 1916, the Battalion paraded and received the "straight wire" from the colonel's own lips that the 44th would embark for active service overseas on the 6th June, 1916.

And the great news was all the more welcome because of the many disappointing false alarms and groundless rumors.

CHAPTER III.

THE VOYAGE TO ENGLAND.

The Battalion embarked on the "A29" (H.M.A.T. Suevic) at Fremantle, and she cast off on the afternoon of June 6th, leaving behind the biggest crowd of people that had ever assembled on a West Australian waterfront. From the ship the wharf appeared to be a blaze of color, and with streamers stretching across the ever-increasing gap between land and ship, flags flying, and handkerchiefs waving, the scene was most impressive. The feelings of the troops were mixed—glad to get away from the routine and monotony of peace training, and yet sorry to see the last of loved ones, perhaps for all time.

The units represented on board the Suevic were the 11th Field Ambulance, 11th Field Engineers (both from the Eastern States), the 44th Battalion and its 1st reinforcements, with a total parade state of about 1600 souls. The ship was uncomfortably crowded, and especially until everyone settled down, there was scarcely room to move. Practically the space available for exercise was only enough for one platoon at a time, so that parades consisted principally of lectures. After the first few days lectures became very stale, and yarns were told instead, and the latter were both entertaining and instructive and produced a very fine crop of imitation Carr Boyds.

There is nothing so monotonous as a long voyage on a crowded troopship. Boat stations and inspections (throat inspections, feet inspections, kit inspections,

THE VOYAGE TO ENGLAND

inspections of quarters, and other inspections, in fact everything but an inn-spection!); these, with sports and concerts, helped to pass the time. Gambling was not officially allowed, but nevertheless the troops played poker for fun and "house" for money. "Don't" is a word the Aussie cannot make friends with.

The Battalion's First Death.

Sickness became prevalent in spite of the good work of the A.A.M.C., and alas, the Battalion had its initial death on board ship. A young lad from Claremont, who had built up quite a reputation for his boxing skill, was the first victim, and the funeral service made a deep impression on everyone. With the ship stopped in mid-ocean—the padre standing over the dead reciting the mournful burial service— all ranks with bared and bowed heads—the bugler's "Last Post"—the firing party's volley—and then the heart-moving splash; and one comrade lived only in the memory of those who had known him in life. The sense of loss was great, and in striking contrast to the impression that even the lengthiest casualty list later on produced.

Time hung heavily. Any strange fish or the spout of a whale was sufficient to draw the attention of all the unoccupied. The most exciting incident was caused through the failure of an ash valve in the bottom of the ship to close, thus causing a leakage. The stoppage of the engines while the crew endeavoured unsuccessfully to pass a sail over the valve was appreciated by the troops, but the advice given by them to the crew as to exactly how the job should be done was not appreciated by the seafaring coves. This accident caused the captain of the vessel to make for Durban instead of carrying out the original intention of first touching at Capetown.

The main employment of the officers throughout the voyage was the censorship of letters. The instructions as to tabooed information were very strict, and as this was probably everyone's first experience of having to curb their natural writing propensities, the job of censoring was an arduous one—particularly so on account of the fact that most of the spare time was filled in to a great extent by writing letters.

Quarantined.

At Durban the ship was quarantined while being patched up by divers, and the troops were only allowed ashore on route marches for exercise under close supervision. Having been for sixteen days cooped up in a crowded ship, this order did not coincide with the views of the troops, and, being Aussies, many of them took French leave.

At Capetown the quarantine stunt was worked again and Battalion route marches were the rule for the three days' stay at this port. Tragedy was barely averted here, as the orders confining the troops to the ship were quite decisive, and guards were posted on the wharves to prevent anyone leaving her. This caused a very mutinous spirit to show itself, and on one occasion no less than three very ugly rushes were made by the troops on board to break through the guard. Serious trouble was only averted by a display of firmness by the officers concerned, and the loyalty shown to these officers by the members of the guard.

After leaving Capetown the voyage continued under worse conditions than before. The Suevic entered the submarine zone, where at night all portholes had to be closed, all lights extinguished except those strictly covered, while no smoking was allowed on deck. By day and night strict watch had to be kept for sub-

THE VOYAGE TO ENGLAND. 21

marines by guards specially detailed for that purpose, and only those who have had the experience of keeping their eyes glued to a sector of sea can know how wearisome this became.

Boat Accommodation.

It was very interesting to know also that the Suevic had only boat accommodation for one-third of the personnel on board! Consequently three boat lists were drawn up giving everyone a place in a boat during one-third of the voyage only—that is for each fortnight of the six weeks' journey. Under the circumstances life was a gamble, and those people who had drawn a boat for the last third of the trip—the fortnight in the submarine zone—were looked upon as fortune's favorites.

Crossing the Line.

was celebrated by the usual ceremony and jollification. Dr. Alex. Juett was Father Neptune, and with his many vassals, instruments of torture, nasty-tasting pills and soaps, he gave all hands something to help them remember the day. Towards the finish the ceremony became a general melee, in which a number of the previous victims tried to give Neptune a dose of his own medicine. The fun was at its height when the tank burst and ended operations.

At St. Vincent the ship stopped for some time for instructions, and then proceeded on the most dangerous portion of her journey from the submarine point of view. However, never a sub. was sighted, and when twenty-four hours out of Devonport a British destroyer sidled up, the "tin fish" was not mentioned in the betting. The destroyer escorted the Suevic for the remainder of the trip, and on July 26 she anchored safely at the end of the long sea voyage —which had lasted just on seven weeks—and most of the boys got their first glimpse of Blighty bathed in the most glorious morning sunshine.

Devonshire in July.

The troops disembarked in the afternoon and entrained at Devonport for Salisbury Plain. The train journey through Devonshire in July was a wonderful sight for sea-sick eyes. It was then realised that the green seen on the English picture targets used in Australia for musketry training purposes existed after all, together with the hedges and the pocket handkerchief fields, which in Australia had been derided as being natural impossibilities. Thoughts on the train journey generally were that Englishmen had much to fight for in such an extremely beautiful country as was then being unfolded before the eyes.

The 44th detrained at Amesbury, and after indulging in a six mile march reached camp (No. 13) at Larkhill, on Salisbury Plain, not far from the old Druid ruins—Stonehenge—on July 26, 1916.

Pte. "Wallie" Browning. Lewis Gunner. One of the "Dags" of the Battalion.

OFFICERS OF THE ORIGINAL 44th BATTALION.

CHAPTER IV.

IN CAMP ON SALISBURY PLAIN.

Camp life in England was similar in routine to that with which the Battalion had become familiar in Australia. There were, of course, more troops congregated on Salisbury Plain than any Australian soldier had seen before, and this made the place very lively. The Plain was a mass of camps and the whole of the Third Division was assembled and settled in quarters there by the end of August, 1916. Training was elementary and the Battalion went through the whole grind once more from recruit drill upwards.

The Lewis Gun.

With the abolition of the machine-gun as an infantry Battalion weapon the Lewis-gun was introduced, and instruction in that wonderful little weapon

---

OFFICERS OF THE ORIGINAL 44th BATTALION.
(See photo on previous page.)

Top Row: 2nd Lt. T. H. Bone, 2nd Lt. R. E. Walsh, 2nd Lt. C. W. Couchman, 2nd Lt. W. H. Cooper, 2nd Lt. W. J. Stables, 2nd Lt. A. A. Guy.

Second Row: Lieut. E. C. Adams, 2nd Lt. G. R. Porter, 2nd Lt. J. E. S. Taylor, Lt. L. T. Hickey, Capt. H. E. Darling, D.S.O., Lt. C. L. Biles, Lt. H. E. Wells, Lt. H. H. Walker, Lt. C. C. Hillary, 2nd Lt. C. Longmore, Capt. A. E. White (Padre).

Sitting: Capt. S. H. Jackson, Capt. W. T. Bryan, Capt. C. H. Lamb, Capt. M. H. A'Beckett, Lt.-Col. W. O. Mansbridge, D.S.O., Major E. Summerhayes, Capt. J. H. Foxworthy, Capt. W. H. Rockliffe, Capt. A. Juett (M.O.), Capt. J. Peat.

Front: 2nd Lt. R. Skinner, 2nd Lt. H. L. Fowler, 2d Lt. D. S. Meares.

was given first to the headquarters section and then to the company sections. In this connection it is interesting to record that towards the completion of the training, tests were conducted under Divisional supervision, and the 44th Lewis gunners topped the list in each of the three competitions between the Lewis-gun representatives of the thirteen Battalions of the Division.

Esprit de "Battalion."

The Battalion at this stage had a definite personality. It was recognised by the individual as his home; it fed him, clothed him, and paid him. As a self-respecting soldier he growled about most things within the Battalion, but outside of it he always spoke and thought of it with genuine feelings of affection. When colors were issued—the oval blue and white—"esprit de Battalion" became the dominating impulse in the lives of the individuals who comprised it, and this "second-to-none" idea lasted right through the eventful history of the Battalion. In other Battalions it was the same; after the Battalion the Brigade, then the Division, and finally in a wider sphere the average Australian soldier was intensely proud of the fact that he belonged to the Australian Corps, though this last became more generally noticeable during the final year of the war, when for the first time all the five Divisions forming the Australian Corps fought side by side in the same battles and under the same commander.

The Bustard Stunt.

After the more or less monotonous routine of individual training and company and Battalion tactical schemes, Brigade operations were commenced. The 11th Brigade was composed of the 41st, 42nd, 43rd, and 44th Battalions, and its commander throughout

IN CAMP ON SALISBURY PLAIN.

was Brigadier-General Cannan, C.B., an officer from the 15th (Queensland) Battalion. The most memorable training scheme in which the Brigade took part was the occupation for three days of a system of trenches at the Bustard (which isn't how the troops pronounced it), a place a few miles from Larkhill. In this stunt everything had to be carried out as though it was an ordinary front line system of trenches and with an imaginary active enemy opposite. The most persistent enemy the Battalion had on this occasion (and it afterwards proved to be the same in France) was the rain. It scarcely ceased during the three days and nights in which the trenches were occupied, and what with that, the strain on the imagination in trying to "make believe" the enemy, the working parties constructing dug-outs and digging trenches and building everything that had ever been built in trench warfare to that date, and the fact that no one excepting "brass hats" were allowed on top, it was no wonder that the troops were heartily glad when the time came for relief. Although the Battalion did not realise it at the time, those three days paved the way very thoroughly for its first "dinkum" tour in the line at a later date.

The Origin of the Term "Digger."

Before marching home again, the Brigadier assembled the whole Brigade and pointed out the various lessons which had been learnt while occupying the trenches. He gave figures compiled from measurements taken by his engineer officers of the amount of digging done by each Battalion. He stressed the fact that the 44th had dug more than the other three Battalions combined, and as in his opinion digging was more important in this war than rifle shooting, he urged those Battalions to try and reach the digging standard of the 44th. As the units of the

Brigade moved off under their respective commanders voices reached the men of the 44th: "Make way for the 'Diggers'!" "Lend us your steam shovels, 'Diggers!'" and many other remarks, some of which were not complimentary. From that time on "Hello Digger!" was the mode of address employed by outsiders when speaking to members of the 44th, spreading thence to other Battalions, and eventually to the whole of the A.I.F. This is the origin (oft-discussed and many times guessed at) of the term "Digger," which is now so universally applied when referring to the Australian soldier.

Major-General John Monash was now in command of the Third Division, and the next big training operation was a Divisional march. In marching order, with cookers, transport, Lewis guns, and all the encumbrances and impedimenta incidental to a military "move," the Division marched 14 miles—twenty thousand men with horses and vehicles in column of route. The head of the column was just returning to camp when the tail started.

More Inspections.

In order to test the fitness of the Division for active service, a Divisional "fit for active service" parade was held. The chief feature of this was the energy and vim of the dozens of staff officers employed inspecting, and the thoroughness with which they carried out their jobs. Woe to the company commander who had allowed one of his men to come on parade with a trouser button missing! His name was taken and his military future was a blank.

The Diggers' "Pow-Wow."

An operation, also for testing purposes, was performed by the 44th Battalion and representatives from the various technical services in the Division.

This was an attack on, the capture of, and the consolidation of a crater. The troops were placed under the command of Lieut.-Colonel Mansbridge, and the stunt was carried out with success before a fine gathering of generals and staff officers. At the finish, of course, the usual "pow-wow" was held. This was intended to be for officers only, but the officiating general, in calling on the before-mentioned staff officers to assemble around him, made it appear that he invited the Diggers over. They came with picks and shovels and caked with mud, and shoulder to shoulder with, and squashed up against, dignified English and amused Australian staff officers, they listened to a very interesting summing up and criticism of their work, in which they frequently had to submit to being called "Gentlemen."

Before leaving England the King reviewed the whole of the troops on Salisbury Plain. The parade marched past in columns of companies and made a wonderfully impressive sight.

Arrival in France.

Time was now getting on. November, 1916, and the 44th Battalion, with the remainder of the Third Division, was fretting under the fact that it was still in England and had been kept there while its four big brothers, the 1st, 2nd, 4th and 5th Australian Divisions, had been fighting heavily in France all through the summer. However, during November the orders came through for overseas, and on the 26th November, 1916, the 44th Battalion moved from No. 13 Camp, embarked for the Channel voyage, and arrived in France on November 27th, 1916.

CHAPTER V.

THE ARMENTIERES SECTOR.

The "Rest" Camp.

The Battalion disembarked at Havre, and after orders, counter-orders, and much confusion generally it was ordered to "San Vic" rest camp, the route being up a gentle rise. This gentle rise (1 in 5) kept its uniformity of slope all the way around a corkscrew road, and when the exhausted troops had done five miles of it they understood the necessity for having a rest camp at the top of a hill! The English officer in charge of the camp had received no instructions to prepare for the Battalion, and he therefore would not issue tents, blankets, or rations. This meant that

The First Night in France.

was to be remembered as one of icy misery, with a bitter wind howling across the top of the hill, and the slush and mud underfoot giving a foretaste of the great influence it was to have over the men's lives during the next two years.

Next morning the orders came through that the Battalion would arrive at the rest camp, so red tape was satisfied, blankets, tents and rations were issued, and everyone made themselves as comfortable during the next two days as was possible under the wintry conditions. Instructions then came through that the Battalion was to move to the forward area. Marching down the hill to the station, the Battalion entrained—40 men (with all equipment and three days'

THE ARMENTIERES SECTOR. 31

rations) to each horse truck. The memories of the next two days and nights in that train linger yet. The cold was so intense that the crowded condition of affairs proved a blessing in disguise.

First Billets in France.

Bailleul was reached at midnight and the troops tumbled into the mud of the railway yard. Two companies were lucky and found motor 'buses detailed to take them to their billets. The other two marched along slippery cobbled roads to Steenwerck, which was reached about 4 a.m. The billeting arrangements had been bungled, and all hands simply lay down on the cobble stones of Steenwerck and cursed the cold and the wet and the staff until daybreak. Then, after much delay, each company was detailed to its billet—some fair, some bad. "A" and "B" Companies were in glass "hot" houses with many panes of glass missing, and only places here and there where no rain could get in. In "A" Company's hot-house the engineers had placed some pontoons. As these pontoons occupied the only dry places in the billet, efforts were made to shift them so as to make the space they occupied available for the Diggers. It was days before authority could be obtained, and the fuss and the care which the department concerned took of those pontoons made the Diggers think that pontoons must be playing a very prominent part in winning the war. Those hot-houses were cold billets. As "B" Company's wag remarked, "The Lord help us if we're ever billeted in a refrigerator!"

In Reserve.

By this time the 9th and 10th Brigades of the 3rd Division were actually in the line. The 11th was in reserve to the other two, and occupied its time by parades, working parties, visits to the trenches by officers and n.c.o.'s, watching aeroplanes—and last but not least, learning French from the Mademoiselles of Armentieres and Steenwerck.

This state of affairs lasted for three weeks, and then the 11th Brigade took over the front line. The sister Battalion of the 44th was the 42nd, and the latter occupied the Epinette portion of the Armentieres sector on December 22, 1916. The 44th then moved from Steenwerck to billets in Armentieres, and from this time active service actually commenced. With working parties to the front line trenches every night, fatigue parties and carrying parties, the time was fully occupied.

The Front Line.

On December 29, 1916, the 44th relieved the 42nd and took over the front line for the first time, moving in for its tour of duty via Lunatic Lane, a communication trench leading from the ruined Lunatic Asylum at Armentieres to the reserve trenches. The Battalion was now in its tenth month of existence as a complete unit, and members had begun to think that they would never see Fritz in his native state. However, for the next twenty-two months they were destined to see more of him than was necessary for the worst glutton in the Battalion.

The sector occupied was flat country dotted with shell holes, and here and there a ruined farm. The "trenches" were mostly breastworks built of sandbags with the floor "duckboarded" for convenience of movement. The communication trenches were "A" framed and revetted, but the dug-out accommodation generally was poor, and simply amounted to improvised shelters from the weather. None of them would stop a direct hit from even the smallest shell. Water was up to the

THE FIRST BILLET IN STEENWERCK.
The Glass "Hot" House.

Pte. "Paddy" Pullen, M.M., Sgt.-Major Sweeney, and Sgt. "Jim" Butler, D.C.M., in the Armentieres sector.

Note.—1. The dug-out (not of concrete). The Australians were **not** masters of the art of building dug-outs. 2. The mud on Jim Butler's putties.

Above is a photo. taken in the Armentieres sector of a German "unter officier" who was killed at Passchendale.

THE ARMENTIERES SECTOR.   35

knees in the duckboarded trenches in many places, while off the duckboards mud reigned supreme. It was almost impossible to drain the water off on account of the extreme flatness of the locality.

It was supposed to be a quiet sector, but the Battalion was afterwards in others which appealed to them as being quieter. The 3rd Division had been in the line for about a month—new troops and full of vim—and they had succeeded in stirring Fritz up until he retaliated with similar vim. Unfortunately for the Diggers, the infantry seemed to be the main target for the artillery of both contestants. If the Australian artillery fired at Fritz's front line, he retaliated—not at the offending artillery, but at the poor old inoffensive infantry in the front line opposite the sector of his own line which was being bombarded. If the Australian trench mortars opened up, so did his, and again the "footsloggers" suffered. It can be imagined, then, with what interest the infantry received the news each day that there would be a "shoot" at a certain time, and the suspense with which they awaited it, and the inevitable retaliation.

"Minnies!"

Fritz in this sector was well supplied with "minnies," a trench mortar shell which "popped" from his line, could be seen going straight up and its flight followed with the naked eye until it came to earth, and, after a pause, burst. It was most in-

---

(See photo on previous page.)
Note.—1. The concrete dug-out. The Germans were masters of the art of concrete construction, the thickness of the walls being anything from three to six feet and giving protection from even the biggest shell. 2. The gas mask container hanging from the neck. 3. The 'Iron Cross' ribbon. 4. The dog. 5. The cigar.

teresting to watch—when not directed at the part of the line occupied by the watcher. Then, of course, it was murder! These "minnies" created a very "windy" feeling. No dug-out in the line would stop one, and the appalling explosion they made, and the tremendous destruction to earthworks and trenches, made them probably the most feared projectile the infantry had to face.

First Battle Casualties.

The first battle casualties of the Battalion were caused by a "minnie" which burst on "B" Company's parapet on December 30, 1916, killing instantly three lads of that company. A coincidence about these first casualties was that the names of the men killed were Anderson, Barker, and Cameron. A grim alphabetical beginning!

Trench Routine.

The Battalion commenced at once the trench routine practised in peace training, and kept it up with minor alterations right through the piece. With the nightfall a patrol would steal out into No Man's Land and perform a set task, such as "examine enemy wire at such-and-such a point," "examine ditch at so-and-so." This patrol remained out for two hours. When it returned another would go out, and this procedure was carried out through all the hours of darkness. The result of this was that the men got very confident in their patrol work, and by denying Fritz the right to patrol freely, kept command of No Man's Land. Patrol duty was certainly risky work, but it suited the Australian temperament, and consequently, there was never any lack of volunteers to carry it out. To the patrolling activity and efficiency of the Australian Corps generally can a fair share of its success be attributed.

The Lighting Contract.

Front line troops were issued with two kinds of flares, one white and the other red. The white flare was for use in case anything suspicious was seen over the parapet, and the red—the S.O.S.—signal was only to be used in order to bring down the Australian artillery on the enemy front line in case of an attack. These flares were poor old things, and they were very seldom used. The German flare, on the other hand, was very bright and hung in the air for quite an appreciable time. He used all the colors of the rainbow and kept them going from dusk until dawn. When it is realised that one of his flares would light up an area of hundreds of square yards as brightly almost as daylight, it can be imagined that the task of the patrols was not too pleasant. If a patrol was moving when a flare was fired its members would stand fast, only inclining the head slightly towards Fritz, and remain motionless until the flare had died down. The German relied on his flares for protection against surprise attack, and the Australians relied on the consistency and initiative of their patrols.

This is not authentic, but the story goes that one night a sentry directed the attention of the officer of the watch to some suspicious object in front of the 44th wire. The officer had two Verey light (flare) pistols, one with a red and the other containing a white light. Said he: "Watch while I put up a bright light," pointing one pistol up and in the direction of the suspicious-looking object, and holding the other at arm's length behind him. Bang! In his excitement he pulled both triggers. The white light hit the parapet a foot in front of his pistol and the red one went through his batman's foot; and the now unmistakable 44th patrol out in front shouted out that they were a ——— windy lot of ———!!

Machine Guns and Rifles.

Machine guns and rifles were quiet by day in this sector, but at night livened up considerably with unaimed fire, and fire from guns and rifles in fixed positions. The casualties caused by the rifle and machine gun were therefore negligible, being confined to an odd working or wiring party. A rifle or machine gun bullet passing fairly close makes a slight hissing sound. On the other hand, the bullet passing high up in the air over a trench gives off a sharp explosive crack, and is apparently much more dangerous than the other. Going up Japan Avenue—a communication trench 10 feet deep—one dark night, an officer caught up with a little runner who had just left Battalion headquarters with a message for one of the companies. A bullet cracked overhead and the runner ducked. A few yards—another crack, another duck. "By ——!" said the runner, "that blasted Fritz has been sniping me all night. I don't know how the devil he spots me, but he does!"

Wiring Parties.

A wiring party did not provide a man with a job which he could enthuse over. In addition to his rifle and ammunition, he carried wire, screw pickets, and a few other odds and ends. On the job, there was a certain amount of unavoidable noise and, as stated previously, Fritz had an unlimited quantity of first-class flares. In addition to the risk of discovery and the consequent aimed machine gun and rifle fire, there was always some stray machine gunner or rifleman having a go for luck.

"Stand To!"

At dawn all hands in the trenches "stood to," as that was generally recognised as the standard time for an attack. Dawn also sometimes brought with it a chance for a shot at some tempting target—a

THE ARMENTIERES SECTOR.

belated straggler from a working party or patrol, or perhaps an incautious sentry.

One of "D" Company's sentries at dawn, looking through field glasses over the parapet, received a bullet obliquely through the glasses. The shock knocked him off the firing step, and when he scrambled to his feet a sergeant wiped the blood from his face, caused by glass splinters, and told him he was a lucky dog. "How about my finger?" asked the sentry, holding up his hand, from which one finger was missing. The sergeant picked up the sentry's glove, shook it, and the finger fell out.

The Battalion occupied the Armentieres sector until March, 1917. Six days in the line and six out—and the "spells" out of the line were looked upon as being almost as bad as the turns in the line—what with working parties and carrying parties up to the front line, which the "resting" Battalion had to supply every night.

That Three Weeks' Cold Snap.

February provided a three weeks' spell of bitterly cold weather. The ground was frozen hard for eighteen inches below the surface, and this made it almost impossible to rebuild any earthworks or trenches which the Hun shells destroyed. The parapet in all cases where it was blown in was temporarily repaired with sandbags of frozen earth, and the day the thaw came these places sagged very low, and so gradually that the happening was not noticed until an opposing sniper had had a snapshot. Life in the front line was almost unbearable. The sentries—wrapped up in mufflers, leather waist-coats, greatcoats, and with fingerless gloves—found their tour of duty to be one of almost intolerable torture. In every little post, composed of half a dozen men, the braziers and fuel for them were most important articles, and the brains that were used in the "wangling" of an extra issue of coke in many cases reached the heights of genius.

The cold was so intense that it even froze on the guns the "non-freezable oil" issued especially for the Lewis gun, with the result that the guns were unworkable until thawed. On this being reported to the authorities, Lewis gunners were issued with an extra ration of coke and instructed to keep the guns in the vicinity of the brazier when not in use.

CHAPTER VI.

THE RAIDS.

The "Little" Raid.

While occupying the Armentieres sector the 44th carried out two raids on the Hun line. The first was a small affair, made up of about 30 men under Captain Biles, and it took place at 6 p.m. on January 10. The raid was well organised, and the raiders had been trained behind the line in the various parts they had to play. Everything went like clockwork. The party assembled in No Man's Land, and at zero hour the barrage came down. Fritz immediately replied on No Man's Land and the 44th front line, and to those unfortunates whose duty it was to man the trenches, it seemed that the whole of the German artillery on the Western front was being concentrated on the sector. With minnies, five-nines, and whiz-bangs, the trenches for the next half-hour rocked and rolled like a ship at sea.

Communication.

In the front line during the course of the bombardment was a very anxious little party—the O/C Raid, his two runners and two signallers, together with one officer and 12 men detailed to stand by as a reserve. One of the signallers was squatted on the floor of the trench with the field telephone to his ear. The other end was out in No Man's Land, and, according to plan, word was to be sent back to the O/C Raid reporting the progress of the raiding party. Prior to the bombardment a message had come through, "Enemy wire not cut." As it had that morning been reported blown to pieces this was a disturbing item of news. During the bombardment the second message was, "Casualties coming back." Then no word for some time. The trench was being shaken with bursting shells, and each one of the little party expected every moment that one would drop in their midst, which would have ended all the petty worries of this world as far as they were concerned. It was almost intolerable to simply have to sit there unable to do a single thing. The O/C's tense voice, "Are they in yet, sig.?" and the "No, sir!" in reply from the quiet signaller, were the only words spoken. Then "Message, sir!" from the signaller. "In!" and a sigh of relief from everyone told how intensely they had awaited that one little word signifying that the raiders had entered the enemy trench. Then the casualties appeared on the parapet, carried by the stretcher-bearers who had gone out with the raiders. These were helped down and passed back. The next message expected was the notification that the party had left the German trenches and were coming back, and anxiety again appeared on all faces while waiting for that message. It came; "Out, sir!" reported the signaller, "and coming back!"

A few minutes later and the raid was over!

The fact that verbal communication could be kept up under the heaviest fire and amid such exciting conditions may seem extraordinary now, especially when it is realised that only 200 yards separated the two front line trenches, and the total time allowed for the raid was only about half an hour. The signaller speaking at one end of the wire was with the O/C assault. He went right on to the enemy parapet, and his telephone wire was twice cut by shell fire, the breaks having to be found instantly and repaired.

THE HOPELESS DAWN.
A Typical "Stand To!" (David Barker in the "**Anzac Book**").

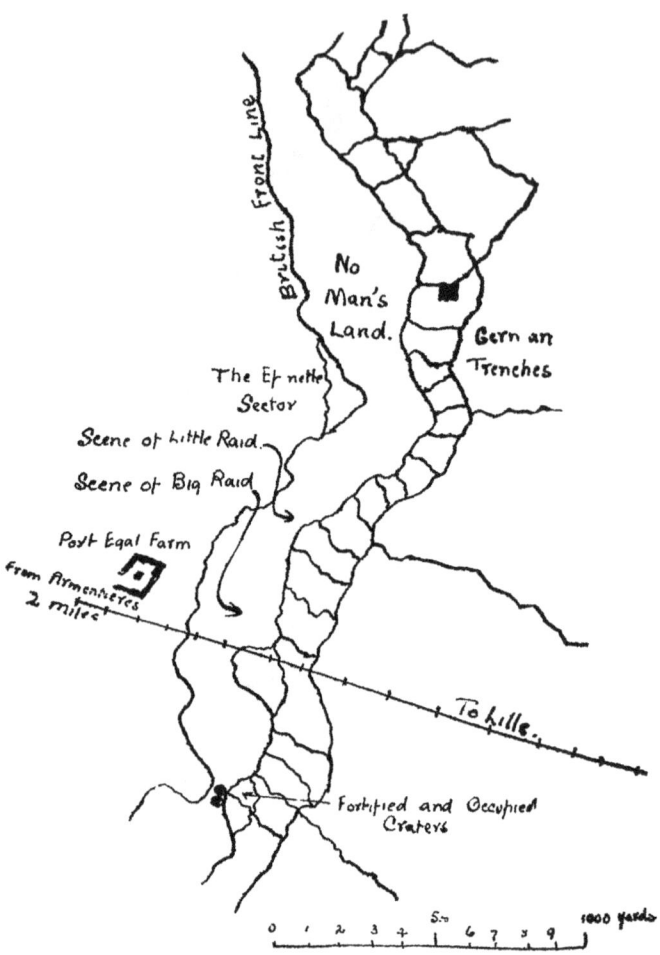

It was a valuable lesson in that practical communication which is the very first essential to success in the field.

*   *   *   *   *   *

The raiding party in the meantime had made their way through the enemy wire and had entered his trenches. These were worked along by bombing and bayonet parties for about fifty yards each way, but never a Hun did they encounter. The raiders then withdrew, Lieut. "Sammy" Taylor bringing back a German sign post to show that the party had not failed in getting in to their objective. The casualties among the raiders were six men wounded. The raid did not succeed in its main object of capturing prisoners, because the enemy evidently expected something and withdrew temporarily. But the one point established was that the representatives of the Battalion had attacked Fritz for the first time, and in spite of all obstacles and shell-fire had entered his line, and the immediate feeling in the Battalion was that what they had done once they could do again when the occasion arose. It was a satisfactory try-out.

The "Big" Raid.

The next raid was on a more ambitious scale, and was carried out on March 13, 1917. The scene

---

(See photo on previous page.)
Rough sketch of the Armentieres sector showing the front line occupied by the 44th Battalion from December 1916 to March 1917. Note: (1) The system of communication trenches between the German front and support lines. The sketch only shows the British front line, but its communication and support trenches were similar to those of the Germans. (2) The forward bend of the German front line on the railway line. (3) The two craters occupied by Fritz and their proximity to the British front line. (4) The scale, which will give an idea of the varying width of No Man's Land.

was a few hundred yards south of that of the small raid, and the party consisted of 6 officers and 400 men under Capt. C. H. Lamb. It aimed at penetrating the enemy first and second lines of defence, working along north for some hundreds of yards, capturing prisoners, and destroying defences. The most complete arrangements were made, even to the construction of dummy trenches in the rear area similar in outline to those being raided, and the practice of the raid over them. The artillery barrage was the heaviest the Third Division had yet employed, and it was augmented by the Army Heavy Group. This Group, let it be explained, at that period was travelling up and down the Army front and worked to a programme limiting its time in each Divisional or Corps area. The said time limit had an important bearing on the subsequent operation.

Mud!

The luck was against the Battalion on this occasion. For days prior to the raid it rained incessantly, and No Man's Land was a mass of mud—with ditches and shell-holes full of water. The whole area was very thoroughly churned up previous to the raid by the artillery and trench mortar fire directed at the enemy wire for the purpose of blowing gaps through it. His artillery retaliated just as actively, and between the two of them it looked as though there was going to be something doing on the Western front. The Hun borrow-ditch (i.e., the wide ditch in front of his trench, from which earth had been shovelled back to strengthen the parapet) was up to twelve feet wide, four to six feet deep, full of water, and lined with barbed wire.

The Search Light on No Man's Land.

While the raiders were assembling (and the assembly of four hundred men in No Man's Land was a

THE RAIDS. 47

big operation in itself) a Hun searchlight, of which there were several in use in this sector, picked them up and then concentrated its rays on No Man's Land about one hundred yards north of the assembling raiders. From the railway line where the German front line bent forward the whole assembly could be seen silhouetted against the rays of the light, and, although no artillery fire was brought to bear then, full information as to what was happening was evidently telephoned back to Hun headquarters—as subsequent events proved. However, without casualties, the assembly of the raiders was completed in perfect order and on time, in spite of the mud and slush which even then made movement very difficult. At midnight the Australian barrage opened on the German front line. Almost immediately the Hun replied with artillery and minnies on to the raiders assembled in No Man's Land. So accurate and sudden was this reply that it was apparent to everyone concerned that the first element of success—surprise—was not with the attackers. According to programme, however, they commenced the move towards the enemy front line. The going was so extraordinarily difficult though that only two parties were able to enter the hostile trenches. One of these parties waded through the borrow-ditch—up to their necks in water, with wire underfoot, and holding Lewis guns and rifles above their heads—and this in the face of a shower of stick bombs thrown by the defenders! Outside of these two parties the remainder were hung up in groups struggling to get through the enemy wire, and the shell fire, machine gun and rifle fire and bomb bursts were so intense, and the mud so gluey, that it was apparent to everyone that success was improbable. Notwithstanding this no one thought of retreat, and with curses at every obstacle, the attackers pressed onward.

Sammy Taylor's Last Order.

Lieut. "Sammy" Taylor was the officer in charge of the assault, and he soon saw that the attack had failed, and to persevere under the awful conditions prevailing would be a further useless sacrifice of life. He therefore gave his last order—the order to withdraw—and anyone knowing Sammy knows that it was the most distasteful order he ever gave. As the order was passed around, the men could hardly believe it. "Retire be d——!" "Who said retire?" "We'll see the —— show right through!" etc. Another voice in reply: "Sammy Taylor said we've got to get back!" And it was only Sammy's name and reputation that caused the order to be obeyed.

Soon after seeing that his order was being carried out, alas! dear old Sammy was killed instantly by a shell.

The Withdrawal.

Now remained a most difficult operation. It required much physical strength and stamina to move about in the morass of No Man's Land, and with dozens of wounded men—their cries and groans, the bursting shells, and the unending rattle of machine guns and rifles—it seemed that the 44th raiders were doomed to destruction. The searchlight still lit up the scene, and with the German flares which were now being sent up in scores, the scene was as bright as day. Unwounded men worked all night long under these terrible conditions bringing in their wounded comrades, and when dawn broke with one exception every wounded man and many of the dead had been brought in. The exception among the wounded was Corporal Ted Herrod, who was badly wounded in the German front line trench and was taken prisoner by them next morning.

THE RAIDS.

Captain Lamb, after receiving word at Raid headquarters that the assault had failed went out into No Man's Land and worked like a Trojan all night getting his wounded in. Lieut. Lintott was another officer who did splendid work in this direction. He made trip after trip across to the enemy wire and, remaining out until dawn, was the direct means of saving many lives. Towards morning he found a man he had been looking for all night, Sgt. Ted Porter, who was badly hit in the spine and was lying in the mud a few yards in front of the Hun wire. When Porter saw Lieut. Lintott he said: "Charlie, I knew d—— well you'd come out and get me, otherwise I'd have chucked in my alley!"

Many n.c.o.'s and men performed deeds that night of heroism and self-sacrifice, all worthy of official mention, but unknown except to a few busily engaged in performing similar actions. Had the weather been even decent, there is no doubt that the raid would have been successful. The plans, the organisation and the execution of all details were well nigh perfect. All ranks were imbued with the spirit of victory, and that the operation failed can only be attributed to one thing, and one only—not enemy shells or machine gun and rifle fire (heavy as they were) but mud, treacherous and slimy mud.

The Responsibility.

In connection with the responsibility for the carrying out of the operation under the prevailing weather conditions, Captain Lamb, as O.C. Raid, pointed out to the Brigadier the necessity for postponing it until a more favorable opportunity presented itself. Whose responsibility it then became is not quite clear, but the reason given for not postponing the operation was that the Army Heavy Group Artillery was due to shift further south, and as they could not alter their programme the raid must go on. If that is correct then whatever individual was responsible for committing 400 men to a hopeless attack against a well-armed and organised position, simply because to do otherwise would interfere with the programme of the artillery, was certainly not a fit man for any position of authority.

Casualties.

The casualties amounted to 20 killed and 45 wounded, and one wounded prisoner of war. Among the killed were men whose death had a deep effect on the Battalion. Lieut. "Sammy" Taylor's death caused widespread grief, not only among his own "C" Company, but throughout the whole Battalion, for he was loved by all who knew him as a soldier and a man. Sergeant "Jimmy" Foy, a well-known Perth athlete, was another soldier whom the Battalion could ill afford to lose.

The A.I.F. Spirit.

Although the raid failed in its object, and heavy casualties were incurred, a wonderful spirit spread through the Battalion as a result of the heroism and self-sacrifice shown by all concerned. Always after that the men went into a fight with the firm conviction that if they were hit they would not be left to lie and die unaided, but that they would be sought for under the worst of conditions by their own comrades, and at any risk to the seekers.

Decorations Awarded.

Several decorations were awarded for deeds performed that night. Captain Lamb and Lieut. Lintott each received the Military Cross, and various n.c.o.'s and men got Distinguished Conduct Medals and Military Medals.

CHAPTER VII.

"PLUGSTREET."

From the Armentieres sector the Battalion side-slipped northwards and took over the Ploegstert Wood sector about the middle of March. The change from the mud of the Epinette locality was a welcome one, especially as the new sector allowed of a great deal of freedom of movement above ground, and out of communication trenches altogether. The firing line skirted the front of the wood itself, and although the timber nearest Fritz was shot to pieces, it gave complete cover from view about one hundred yards behind the front line trenches or breastworks. The accommodation was much better than Armentieres, there being several concrete machine gun posts and dugouts. Strange to say, the Lewis gunners made very little use of their concrete gun dug-outs, excepting to sleep in. They preferred the open parapet and its freedom of action and view.

Rats!

The Diggers appreciated Plugstreet. The rats (not mentioned before but very plentiful in the Armentieres sector) were numerous, hungry and cheeky. From the support line in the wood snipers improved their shooting with revolvers and rifles by firing at rats foraging in the wood in front of the support line. This at last brought verbal and hasty requests from the front line garrison, couched in fiery Aussie language, and to the effect that they did not mind that which was expected to come from their front, but that the shooting from the rear must stop at once or there'd be another war!

The "Birdcage."

Plugstreet was a curious line. In the centre of the sector was a locality called the "Birdcage." The front trenches there formed a rectangle, with Fritz's front line in prolongation to that of the 44th. How it happened the Battalion never definitely knew, but the legend ran that when the two armies sat down to trench warfare in the early days of the war, the Hun made a small attack and captured part of the British front line between two communication trenches. In spite of frequent attempts he refused to be pushed out, and eventually the British converted the two communication trenches and the support line between them into a new front line. They sprung two mines under the original front line, and Fritz also exploded a couple. The result was that two portions of the old front line were blown out of existence, but Fritz obstinately hung on to the remnants, and by digging two trenches across old No Man's Land he connected up with his own original front line trench. No tactical reason could be assigned for his obstinacy, as the ground was flat and gave no special advantage to the holder. An estaminet had once stood on the spot, but it had long ceased to exist, except as a heap of powdered stones.

The Steel Tree.

In this portion of the front line also was a steel tree with a foundation of concrete. The original tree stood on the edge of Plugstreet Wood, and had been cut off by a shell about 15 feet from the ground. Measurements were taken, and a tree of steel constructed behind the lines. A concrete foundation

THE R.A.P. (REGIMENTAL AID POST) IN THE ARMENTIERES SECTOR.

The top figure is Capt. Kenihan, M.C., the South Australian medical officer who was attached to the 44th during its first twelve months in France. He was awarded the M.C. for services rendered at the Battle of Messines. As can be seen from the photo R.A.P.'s in the line were hardly the spacious and convenient surgeries which are familiar to civilian life, but all classes of operations were performed in them, and generally with very great success, if not comfort, to the casualty.

"PLUGSTREET" WOOD.

AN AEROPLANE PHOTO. OF THE "BIRDCAGE" AT PLUGSTREET.

was put in a few feet from the original tree, and when all the numerous details had been attended to, it was cut down at night and the steel imitation erected in its stead. It was a wonderful imitation too, the outside appearance and the splintered top having been so faithfully reproduced as to deceive at first anyone, even in the British front line, who was not a very close observer. It was possible to climb a ladder inside and view the enemy trenches through a wire mesh loophole with sliding steel shutters. All shoots were observed from it. The only drawback was the draught (which caused every bone in the body of the observer to ache), and the smell, the latter being caused by the stagnant water collected at the foot, which could not be drained away.

Pinching Fritz's Assembly Tape.

In Plugstreet, of course, the usual trench routine was carried on. The whole life of the Digger now consisted of "days of monotony, punctuated by moments of intense fear." The shell that landed near enough to any man to make him "duck," "put the wind up him" for the moment, even if he did laugh afterwards. Patrolling at night afforded many opportunities for the enterprise and initiative of the

---

AN AEROPLANE PHOTO. OF THE "BIRDCAGE" AT PLUGSTREET.
(See photo on previous page.)

Note.—1. The curious conformation of the two front lines. 2. The craters. 3. The dead and stagnant appearance of No Man's Land compared with the area inside the two front lines. 3. The miles of trenches. 4. The shellholes. 5. The two moated farms, one with Fritz's front line running through it, and the other just behind the 44th front line. The latter was called Hull's Burnt Farm, and was the extreme right flank of the Battle of Messines in June, 1917.

scouts. The Battalion had not been raided by Fritz in the Armentieres sector, although the sister Battalion had there lost one or two prisoners to enemy raiding parties who succeeded in entering their trenches. At Plugstreet the 42nd chaps were raided again, and although the enemy party got in they took no prisoners, owing to the stout resistance of the defenders. The 44th scouts on one occasion brought back several entrenching tools and stick bombs from a shallow trench, which Fritz had dug for an assembly position in No Man's Land. The next night they found a tape, which had evidently just been laid by some venturesome Fritz patrol, leading from the beforementioned trench to a gap in the 44th wire. This tape was brought in, and the Battalion being relieved the same night, the 42nd then had the bad luck to have the raid put over on them. However, Fritz didn't get in this time, and his raiding party received a very rough handling, as when the S.O.S. was sent up a heavy Australian barrage was concentrated on No Man's Land, and the machine and Lewis guns swept the raiding area with a terrific hail of lead. Next morning two or three dead Germans were visible in No Man's Land, and the "O. Pips" (observation posts) reported much activity by stretcher parties in his lines.

Gas!

The Battalion received its first issue of "dinkum" gas shelling here in March. A German prisoner previously captured had stated that they were later going to use a new gas shell which would absolutely wipe the British out, and thus end the war. Plugstreet, probably on account of the wood (where gas is more effective because it does not dissipate so quickly as in the open), was the sector selected for the Hun experiment. During the whole of one night trench mortars poured these gas shells into the 44th line. Twenty-one mortars were counted in action over 2000 yards of front, and it was estimated that they fired 7000 shells between dusk and dawn. The result was a triumph for the British box respirator (gas mask) and a tribute to the gas training and discipline of the Battalion. Two or three men were affected by the gas, and these, marvellous to relate, were the only casualties. A tour of the trenches next day disclosed the fact that the Hun shooting had been excellent, as the front line and communication trenches were pitted everywhere with shell bursts, and the wonder then was not so much the very few gas casualties, but that half the Battalion had not received direct hits and splinters.

Staniforth Smith.

A man in a gas mask is a grotesque looking object at any time. Lieut. Staniforth Smith (once of the Senate, and later of New Guinea fame) when the shelling first started came into headquarters dug-out with the very praiseworthy intention of giving the alarm. Three or four officers were sitting around a table smoking and doing various jobs. When Staniforth swung back the gas curtain he had the mouthpiece of the mask in his mouth, and was holding his nose with his finger and thumb. He muttered "Gas!" The others looked up, and with one accord burst into a roar of laughter. Staniforth angrily pulled his mask off and told them with no uncertain voice that they could all be gassed to —— before he would ever warn them again, and then he went out into the night —with his mask off!

"They Always Fizz Before They Go Off."

Captain Peat, of "C" Company, who had only recently been through a gas school, picked up a dud gas shell early in the evening (gas officers were noted for their curiosity, as also were bombing officers about bombs), and took it into his company headquarters. It was a pretty shell, bright and shiny, about 3 inches in diameter and perhaps a foot long, and apparently harmless. He examined it carefully, then placed it under his bunk and sat down to write a report on it. Hearing a slight fizzing noise, he looked at the shell and noticed white liquid bubbling through a hole in the nosecap. Remembering the Bairnsfather sketch "They always fizz before they go off" he grabbed the shell, held his breath and his nose, and hurled it into the night.

Aussies as Archaeologists.

Digging in the Plugstreet sector was the main recreation for the "Diggers." Looking back, it was probably the same right through the war. If the Australian Corps had had as much practice with the rifle as they had with the pick and shovel, what a wonderful team of sharpshooters would there be in Australia to-day! While digging one new trench in the wood, "B" Company unearthed about fifty silver and copper coins, the date being that of the eleventh century.

The wire in and around Plugstreet Wood is also worth mentioning. It was pretty well wired when the 44th went there, but when they left it was almost impossible to move anywhere off a duckboard track. Every tree was connected with its neighbour, and what with the miles of loose wire scattered in between it became a toss up as to whether it was there to keep the enemy out or the defenders in.

There were rough wooden crosses dotted all over Plugstreet Wood, and they were inscribed with the names and units of almost every Regiment in the

British Army. The dead were probably buried in the early days where they fell, and by the number of graves representing Battalions already famous in British history, and the fact that there were also many crosses erected to German dead, the fighting there must have been at close quarters, and of a bitter nature, and those units must have added considerable glory to their old records.

The Old Log Hut and Bairnsfather.

A log hut towards the rear of the Wood had been used by most of the previous Battalions as a headquarters. It was there that Bairnsfather made his first sketch, the forerunner of a series of battlefield pictures that were destined to play a very important part in the upkeep of the nation's morale, both at home and in the field. In that hut also each Battalion had left its Regimental Crest, carved or painted on wood. It would be interesting to know what happened to the hut and its contents in 1918 when the Germans captured the Wood; certainly it would have made a splendid site for, and a nucleus of, a war museum.

This sector was occupied until May. Rumors were then plentiful about an approaching "stunt." It could be seen that some big operation was coming off by the increased activity of artillery, aeroplanes and staff officers. At any rate, the Battalion was withdrawn from the line during May, and ordered to move to an area near St. Omer to rest and train for the forthcoming battle.

The March Back.

The 44th Battalion will remember the march back. For six months they had been in the line—six days in and six out. By the constant use of gum-boots (i.e., a rubberised waterproof boot with the uppers extending to the thighs and kept up by an attachment to the belt), and the fact that when gum-boots were not worn, ordinary boots were nearly always soaked through, the men's feet had softened and were quite unfitted for long marches. In spite of that, the first day's march allotted was about 22 miles, to which something was added owing to a staff mistake, and this caused a circle to be marched around Steenwerck. For a first day's march over cobblestones with full packs it was a veritable killer, and getting dizzy going around Steenwerck, with the church spire in the centre and seemingly the same distance away for hours, loud and deep were the Diggers' curses. The worst-tempered Battalion in the A.I.F. lay down in their billets that night! The second day was also very severe, but on the third, with the promise of a decent spell in billets at the end of it, the Battalion got back to normal, and finished up in the best billets that it had yet had in France. Headquarters and "A" Company were at the village of Senighem, and "B," "C" and "D" at Columby, and with barns and farm buildings for quarters all hands were made fairly comfortable, and a fortnight's enjoyable rest, with no fear of an unwelcome visitor in the shape of a minny or five-nine, was entered upon.

CHAPTER VIII.

PREPARING FOR MESSINES.

More Squad Drill.

After six months living under the possibility of meeting death suddenly or of being maimed and mutilated, the sense of relief even to the most devil-may-care was very great, the more so as it was suppressed. The ordinary peace-time parades were held, and training even went back to the old squad drill and rifle exercises. This was very necessary for various reasons. In the first place trench life did not improve parade ground discipline, and the Battalion needed a good tonic to tighten and smarten the whole organisation. In the second, the officers and n.c.o.'s at the end of six months in the line were, owing to the casualties incurred, in most cases new to their present jobs, and there were many of both those ranks who were not confident in commanding men out of the line, although quite competent for the charge of the same men in the line. Although the parade ground training was recognised as necessary still the old soldier privilege of a good grouse was well exercised.

"Le Petite Garcons."

In addition to parades, football matches, sports and concerts were organised, and these provided a very welcome mental change from the purely military side of the life. A children's sports meeting and picnic arranged by Captain "Willie" Bryan was evidently the event of the year to the mothers and children of Columby and Senighem. Although Battalions had been billeted in the village off and on for two years not one had thought of an event like this, and of all the happy days these people had spent surely this particular one was the happiest. The kiddies, with their hands and faces sticky with sweetstuffs and the mothers all brought together for a good old gossip—with games and side-shows—made a memorable day in the history of Columby.

The Brigade now practised the attack on Messines ——"Magnum Opus," as it was called officially—over a system of shallow trenches made as much like the enemy system at Messines as possible. Everything possible was explained to the men, and officers were brought together for conference after conference. For three weeks this rather monotonous training went on, and then the Battalion received orders to move back to the line. On the march back the steel helmets were ordered to be worn, and at the end of a day's march each of these helmets weighed one ton. At 8 p.m. on the third evening, having marched seventeen miles that day, billets were reached at Pont Neippe. At 11 p.m. orders were issued to company commanders detailing various working parties.

Breakfast at 2 a.m.

Some companies had to commence their tasks at 6 o'clock next morning at Plugstreet Wood, and this meant breakfast at 2 a.m., a six miles march before starting work, and a six mile march back to billets when finished.

Under such circumstances the lot of the Company Sgt.-Majors who imparted the good news to the Diggers (already tired and mostly asleep in their billets) was not to be envied.

The Balloon at Pont Neippe.

Pont Neippe at this time was crammed full of Aus-

A TYPICAL TOUR OF DUTY.

"Gawd help the first bloomin' Fritz I see to-night."
—"Anzac Book."

THE 44th GUN SECTION.

tralian troops. Although within easy shelling range of the Hun artillery, for some reason he only sent over odd shells, although his aeroplanes must have seen and reported the crowded state of the town. A spectacular event was the bringing down of a British observation balloon just outside Pont Neippe by a gallant Hun airman. He came over late one evening, and despite a tremendous barrage from the anti-aircraft guns he dived, fired and missed. Circling around again he came back and made no mistake with his second try, as the balloon burst into flames and came down; the occupants, who had jumped out, being let down safely by parachute. The airman then ran the gauntlet of the barrage back to

THE 44th GUN SECTION.
(See photo on previous page.)

The above photo. shows 30 original members of the 44th Gun Section, taken at Claremont in 1916. Eleven of these were killed in action (an exceptionally heavy proportion), and with one exception every other man was wounded once, twice, or three times, which is much greater than the ordinary percentage of casualties which the A.I.F. suffered. Five of them were killed in the Paschendale fighting between October 4 to 21, 1917. They were Sergt. Harry Thrum, Sergt. L. Bysh, Corp. H. Vincent, Lance-Corp. W. Stephens, and Pte. A. Mullins. The others to lose their lives at various places and periods were:—Sergt. L. Jones, Privates Hec. Wade, Short, McNeece, and Boxhall (the latter three were close comrades and were killed by the one shell at Messines), Sergt. P. Blick, and Sergt. Bob Casey (who is not shown in the above photo). Davies, Thorn, Parks, Casey and Rogers obtained their commissions, and in addition Davies received the M.M. and Rogers and Casey the M.C. Sergt. Fraser also got the M.M. The section was split up in France and divided among the companies in consequence of a change in the organisation. That they were genuine battlers and worthy upholders of the machine-gun traditions of the 16th, 11th and 28th their fine record shows.

his own lines, and of the thousands of Aussie soldiers who saw the whole thing the general opinion was that he was a good sport and deserved to get away.

Working parties constructing the hundred and one engineering jobs required for the coming offensive were now the rule. By night the cobbled roads resounded with the rattle of traffic, and the 44th now, if never before, realised the immensity of the preparation necessary for the carrying out of a modern battle.

The Catacombs.

About the beginning of June the Battalion moved from Pont Nieppe and took over the catacombs, a huge system of dug-outs constructed by Australian Tunnellers in Hill 63 in front of Messines. In the main dug-out were quartered the 44th Battalion, H.-Qrs. 11th Brigade, and a number of other details to a total of about 1500 men. It was well ventilated, but as Fritz had the habit of gas shelling Hill 63 at intervals, and the gas curtains were then dropped, it at times became very close and stuffy.

A Dud!

Many curious shell-fire incidents happened here. The cookers were dug into the hill, but even so they had very little protection. One dud shell (5.9) landed in "A" Company's cookhouse fire. Of course, the cooks disappeared, but no explosion following, they came back and investigated. The shell had hit a piece of railway iron upon which the dixies were resting, and had bent it to the shape of a right angle. Why it did not explode was a mystery.

Another one went right through a covered motor-'bus, which stopped for a few minutes at Hyde Park corner, at the foot of Hill 63. It exploded and blew the driver into the road and fearfully mangled a man

PREPARING FOR MESSINES.

ins.de. To make matters worse the explosion splashed petrol all over the 'bus, and in a few seconds it was a roaring mass of flame. The driver picked himself up, and with the assistance of Sgt. Jim Butler managed to let down the door at the back of the 'bus, and to get the wounded man out. While this was being done, the cartridges in some equipment hanging in the fore part of the vehicle were exploding with a rattle as of a machine gun. In addition, the smoke and blaze attracted more shell fire, and for ten minutes or so matters were very lively. The wounded man only lived a few minutes after arrival at the dressing station.

The "Impossible" Job.

While in the catacombs working parties were the order of the day and night—mostly night. The nine days' barrage prior to the Battle of Messines was in full blast, and the Australian line was plentifully plastered with Hun shells in return. One task set the Battalion provided them with some strenuous work in removing about 100 gas cylinders from the front line, where the wind had not been favourable for their discharge towards Fritz. It had previously been reported to Division that it was impossible to move these cylinders owing to the state of the trenches and the constant artillery fire. However, despite its "impossibility," the Diggers removed the last one after three nights' hard work. Hostile shells had even burst and half buried some of these cylinders, and they had to be dug out by the men working in gas helmets. As each cylinder was a heavy load for two men and the carrying distance was nearly two miles—what with shell fire, gas, crooked, broken and narrow trenches—it can be imagined that the Battalion was up against a stiff proposition, and that it was successfully accomplished can only be attributed to the determination and pluck of the Diggers themselves.

The Daylight Raid.

On June 4 sudden orders were received that the 44th were to raid the enemy trenches in front of Messines at 2 o'clock that afternoon. Preparations were hurriedly completed, and ten men from each company made up the raiding party to 40 men, under Lieuts. Lintott and Gaze. The barrage (the nine days' barrage was still in full swing) was timed to lift from the enemy front line at 2 p.m., lengthen on to his support line, and return to his front line at 2.20 p.m. This left the raiders 20 minutes to complete their job—that was, to capture at least one prisoner.

The raiding party went over in two groups, and the very audacity of the operation gained them success, even though it was at a heavy price. They killed many Germans, above ground and in dug-outs, chased others from his front posts to his support line, and captured and brought back five prisoners. Unfortunately the raiding party lost heavily, as Fritz put up a stiff resistance, so much so that of the two officers and 40 men who took part one officer was wounded and 26 men were killed or wounded. The uninjured officer, Lieut. Lintott, of "C" Coy., had a narrow escape, as a rifle bullet scored along the side of his steel helmet and knocked him out for about five minutes.

The A.I.F. Spirit.

This little stunt bristled with examples of the heroism and self-sacrifice which characterised the men of the A.I.F. Sgt. W. Quayle, of "B" Company,

PREPARING FOR MESSINES.

after getting safely back to his own lines with a prisoner, enquired for a particular chum, and was informed that he had been hit on Fritz's wire. Without any hesitation he "hopped the bags" again and set out to look for him. Just as he found him an enemy sniper shot him through the neck, and he fell alongside his mate. Both of them were brought in that night, and although badly wounded both recovered. For his very gallant action Quayle was awarded the Military Medal. Several other decorations were awarded, including a Military Cross to Lieut. "Rick" Gaze, of "D" Coy., who had received during the course of the raid a bullet through his arm.

Zero hour for the Battle of Messines was to be 3.10 a.m. on June 7. At that hour mines were to be exploded under the enemy line; the full barrage was to come down, and after a few minutes the infantry were to attack. The 44th Battalion, with the rest of the 11th Brigade, formed the Third Divisional reserve, and was only to be used in case of any hitch in the programme of the assaulting Brigades, the 9th and 10th.

The Assembly of the 9th and 10th.

The assembly of the 9th and 10th Brigades was carried out under very heavy shell fire, both gas and high explosive. Notwithstanding this, according to plan time, both Brigades were in position, and as far as the Third Division was concerned everything was in readiness for the actual opening of the greatest battle of the war up to that date.

In Reserve!

The 44th Battalion was held in reserve in the catacombs, and according to plan would be the first Battalion of the 11th Brigade to be used in case assistance was required by the assaulting Brigades.

That last night in the catacombs was a wretched experience for all who were unfortunate enough to be confined within its depths. In the first place, Fritz was sprinkling gas shells over the whole area, and this meant that the gas curtains had to be kept down all night. With fifteen hundred men enclosed and no ventilation, it can be imagined that it was something like the Black Hole of Calcutta. The fact that Messines was mined by the British also gave rise to the thought in everyone's mind that it was quite possible for Fritz to have mined Hill 63. It can be realised then that the 44th do not look back on their stay in the catacombs on Hill 63 with feelings of delight. The 44th heard unofficially afterwards that the catacombs were mined by Fritz, but no confirmation was ever received of the rumor. It would be interesting now to know the true facts.

CHAPTER IX.

THE BATTLE OF MESSINES.

With a roar and concussion which shook every timber in the catacombs, the mines went off, the barrage came down, and to those watchers in the trenches on top of Hill 63 a wonderful sight presented itself. Dawn was just breaking, and the ruins of Messines and the defensive works on the forward slopes of the ridge seemed to be a raging tornado of smoke, dust and flame, with spiteful flashes everywhere through it. It seemed to an onlooker that it was absolutely impossible that even a rat should live through that barrage. In addition to the artillery there was a machine-gun barrage involving the use of indirect fire, which was so arranged that from the time the fight started until the objectives were gained, a hail of machine-gun bullets swept along the front and advanced about 200 yards in front of the Australian infantry. This was extraordinarily effective. In one trench the defenders were afterwards found dead in a row, killed not by the morale-wracking artillery fire, but by the invisible stream of deadly machine-gun bullets.

Signs of Success.

As the light improved and the barrage moved forward, the infantry of the 9th and 10th Brigades, like so many ants, could be seen dribbling slowly but surely into the Hun territory. Soon, lightly wounded Diggers came walking back; then came squads of Bosch prisoners with an escort of perhaps a couple of wounded Diggers, who moved nonchalantly at the head and flank of the little column. Now the stretcher parties started to come in, some wounded being carried by the regimental stretcher-bearers and others by German prisoners pressed into a last battle-field duty. The number of prisoners alone answered any question as to whether the attack was succeeding or not.

Sitting on Hill 63, or in the catacombs, was irritating indeed. Reports came through that the attack had been successful, and that, after all, the 44th's part in the great battle would merely be the taking over of the trenches after the attacking troops had consolidated.

However, at 8 p.m. that evening Colonel Mansbridge received orders to retake at dawn the next morning a portion of the Green Line (the furthest objective), which had been evacuated by the attacking Australians. The Battalion was to assemble at Snitchell's Farm, a point in the enemy's line of the previous day, and from there move forward through the troops on the Black Line to their objective, the Green Line.

The Approach March.

At midnight, June 7-8, the Battalion, in single file, left the catacombs for its entry into its first big fight. The approach march was through smashed trenches, with odd gas shells falling and with frequent alarms causing gas helmets to be adjusted, across old No Man's Land, over the trickle called the Douve River, and into enemy territory of the day before. The Australian trenches and positions were bad enough with wreckage and debris, but the Hun front and support lines were blown right out of existence. His

Some "B" Company Diggers Outside their Billet in Columby.

BOSCH FIELD GUN DISABLED AND CAPTURED AT THE BATTLE OF MESSINES.
Note 1. The direct shell hit received on the gun shield.
2. The two rough and typical battlefield crosses erected just in rear of the gun.

A BATTLEFIELD BURIAL.
The grave of Lance-Corporal J. Moyle, "D" Coy., 44th Battalion. Killed in action at Hamel on July 4, 1918.

The Grave of Sgt. J. L. Jones in Armentieres Cemetery.

concrete machine-gun emplacements, however, were generally speaking not much damaged, owing to their enormous thickness and strength.

This approach march was a very difficult operation. It was a fairly dark night, and as the ground had been won only that day no one had had an opportunity of making a thorough reconnaissance. It is not to be wondered at, then, that the companies got mixed and some got temporarily lost before they reached the assembly position. However, in spite of the confusion caused by loss of touch and direction, darkness, and the debris and obstacles which abounded, the four companies and headquarters details were safely assembled in shell-holes near Snitchell's Farm by 2.30 a.m. Notwithstanding all efforts to locate them, no troops could be found on either flank.

The Advance.

The order of the companies in the advance was to be "C" Company under Captain Rockliffe on the left, "A" Company under Captain Bryan on the right, "B" in rear of "C" Company, and "D" Company under Captain Biles in reserve near Snitchell's Farm. Before the Green Line was reached the plan was that "B" Company should move through "C" Company and take the furthest objective, the Green Line. At 3 a.m. the Battalion, spread over an area as platoons in artillery formation, moved forward.

The Grave of Sgt. J. L. Jones in Armentieres Cemetery.
(See photo on previous page.)

Sgt. Jones was the first member of the original 44th Machine Gun Section to be killed. He was bandaging a wounded comrade at the head of Plank Avenue, in the Epinette sector, when an enemy ''pine apple'' exploded, killing him instantly without further wounding the man whom he was attending to.

Enemy shelling now was fairly heavy in response to the Australian barrage, and the accuracy with which the Hun shells fell among the advancing platoons seemed uncanny. Evidences of the severity of the previous day's fighting were now very apparent —wreckage everywhere, dead bodies, Australian and German, with the latter in places piled in heaps. The smell of gas still hanging over the whole area parched the throat and gave everyone a dry choking feeling, and made them gasp for breath.

The Defensive Flank.

The 44th passed through the Black Line in front of Bethlehem Farm. It was held fairly heavily, and the occupants of the shallow trenches had evidently been through a very trying time. Touch with the 4th Division on the left had not been obtained at the assembly position by the 44th, nor could their flank be found during the advance. Consequently Captain Rockliffe with "C" Company, after getting to the position where "B" Company was to leapfrog through them, and having both his flanks in the air in a position which would leave him helpless if attacked, decided to withdraw out of the network of old German trenches, and dig a new and temporary line in the rear. "B" Company meeting "C" Company coming back then moved over to the left and bent their left flank back to the Black Line, thus forming a defensive flank and protecting the flank of the Third Division.

The Gap in the Line.

In the meantime "A" Company, under Captain Bryan, had lost touch with "C" Company, and the position when "B" and "C" Companies started to dig was that the left flank was safe, but there was a gap between "C" and "A" Companies. This gap took a lot of adjusting. "A" Company had two of their

THE BATTLE OF MESSINES.

four officers killed and one wounded, and the casualties among their sergeants were also very high (as a matter of fact, in that unlucky Company only one officer and one sergeant got through the three days unscathed).

"D" Company Fill the Breach.

The position in the centre was therefore so obscure that Colonel Mansbridge ordered "D" Company up to fill the gap, and they moved up through a heavy barrage, which caused them many casualties. They however, got into the required position, and immediately commenced to dig.

The shell fire generally at this time was only moderately heavy, but enemy machine gun and rifle fire was very brisk and accurate. An enemy 'plane came over early, and evidently got the new position, as shortly after it went back the artillery fire became more accurate and caused many casualties among the digging troops.

The Green Line.

Later in the day it was found that the 4th Division was well forward on the left flank, and the 44th at once left their positions and moved up into line, having many men killed and wounded in doing so. This new position was the Green Line, and consolidation was at once begun.

Shellfire!

The enemy located the new positions almost immediately, and concentrated a tremendous artillery barrage on them in an effort to cause another withdrawal. For eleven hours the digging troops endured this rain of projectiles, which lasted well into the night before it slackened. When dawn came the 44th was a tired Battalion, but every man was well dug in.

The next morning, the 9th June, Fritz counter-attacked without success. His troops were caught by the Australian artillery barrage and melted away without reaching the 44th trenches. During the night the line was improved wherever necessary, and patrols pushed out in order to get information as to the whereabouts of the enemy's advanced posts. Artillery fire was consistent all night, and the stretcher-bearers had a strenuous time.

The Relief.

On the 10th June, nothing happened during the daylight hours excepting the inevitable heavy shellfire, which fell upon the 44th trenches with monotonous regularity all day. Towards dusk the 43rd Battalion, advancing to relieve the 44th, were probably seen by Fritz, for he subjected the trenches to another tremendous barrage, and gave the 44th an enthusiastic farewell and the 43rd a warm welcome. Many more casualties were incurred by the troops getting out. Fritz, in addition to the front lines, was bombarding the rear area with much vigour.

Casualties.

The casualties sustained by the Battalion in successfully carrying out its part in its first major operation were 4 officers and 70 men killed and 250 all ranks wounded, out of about 700 men engaged.

Captain "Willie" Bryan.

Many good officers and men went West. Captain "Willie" Bryan, one of the finest officers in the Battalion, was killed on the evening of the first day. No more cheery optimist than he when things were bad was ever in France. An efficient officer, a fine soldier, and a man, "Willie" Bryan's death was mourned by every individual in the Battalion.

THE BATTLE OF MESSINES.

The S.B.'s.

The stretcher-bearers in this battle (as a matter of fact, it was never otherwise) deserve the honor of first mention for individual exploits. Private Opie, of "B" Company, was one who from start to finish thought nothing of his own skin. After doing wonderful work and saving many lives, he attempted to reach a wounded man in an exposed position. Three other stretcher-bearers had tried before him, and two had been killed and one wounded by an enemy sniper. Opie never even hesitated, and went out into the open on his errand of mercy. He was immediately sniped and badly wounded. For his general work throughout the operations and that deed in particular he was recommended for the Victoria Cross, but was awarded instead the next best honor, the D.C.M.

Pte. "Lofty" Pearson's work also deserves mention. Right throughout the existence of the Battalion "Lofty" was a stretcher-bearer, and in that capacity probably carried more casualties off the field of battle than any other man in the 44th. He received the M.M. and bar.

"Doc." Kenihan.

Another whose work was recognised by an award of the Military Cross was "Doc." Kenihan, the medical officer attached to the 44th Battalion. His R.A.P. consisted of a big shell-hole near Snitchell's Farm, and the only protection it had was a few sheets of galvanised iron over the top. Snitchell's Farm and the vicinity was as heavily shelled as the front line, and many narrow escapes did the doctor and his splendid little medical section have.

Other Decorations.

Other decorations awarded were M.C.'s to Captain W. H. Rockliffe, O/C "C" Company; Captain L. Biles, O/C "D" Company; Lieut. Roy Skinner (who carried on with "B" Company after its O/C had been wounded); and Lieut. Pitman, the signalling officer, whose effective work in keeping up communication under the heavy shell fire well earned him the honor. Several D.C.M.'s and M.M.'s were also awarded to n.c.o.'s and men.

Incidents.

Several extraordinary incidents occurred during the course of this operation. One Lewis gunner was killed during the advance by a shell which landed directly underneath him and tossed him twenty feet into the air. He retained the grip of his rifle until he came to earth with a sickening thud—of course, stone dead. Several officers, n.c.o.'s and men were killed and wounded by sniping shots on the first day, and the whereabouts of the snipers was a mystery. On the second day a 44th officer was moving above ground behind the front line and passed close by a heap of German dead. His runner was following him at a distance of about thirty yards, and just as the runner got level with the bodies one of them raised his head and stealthily aimed his rifle at the officer in front. In a few seconds the runner's bayonet had put him beyond the reach of further temptation. Investigation proved that he had been wounded, but had shammed dead, and had evidently done a considerable amount of sniping, as many empty shells were found lying close to his body. This was just in front of Bethlehem Farm, and three 44th officers were sniped and killed in the vicinity.

Rest.

The Battalion next day, sadly reduced in numbers, moved to a rest camp at Neuve Eglise. Two days later it moved to the village of Doullieu to reorganise, refit and train for further rough work ahead.

CHAPTER X.

THE 19 DAYS' STUNT.

While the Battalion rested and reorganised after its trying experiences, the front beyond Messines was pushed forward about a mile, and after the attacking troops had obtained their objectives the job of digging and holding the new front line fell on the 44th. Therefore June 23rd found them wending their way slowly over the broken ground of the Messines Ridge back to the line.

Gapaard.

The new position ran roughly in a line from the left bank of the Lys, near Warneton, to a small ruined village called Gapaard. As taken over, the line was only a series of outpost positions, which had to be turned into one continuous front line trench, with the necessary support and communication trenches.

For the first few days the work was continuous. A desultory shell fire was kept up by the enemy, which, though not heavy, made every man see the necessity for using his pick and shovel to the best advantage. After two days the trenches were decent and averaged six feet in depth, and over the whole Battalion front they had good traverses and firebays. Then began the wiring parties' job of securing these trenches against enemy counter-attacks—this work, of course, being done at night.

FRENCH BOYS PLAYING "TWO-UP."
Forbidden by the authorities, the Diggers still managed to bet the humble franc on a little game of "two-up." Evidently they had their imitators, as the above photo. shows.

"SOMME" COUNTRY.
Game was plentiful on the Somme early in '18. The Diggers had to defend themselves against the concerted attacks of the "wild" poultry which infested the vicinity of the deserted farmyards.

Every Digger who sees this photo. is permitted for the next five minutes to express his opinion on the Great War in general and HIS OWN worst stunt in particular. Language to be limited and chosen according to circumstances at the moment of reading.

Flanders Mud.

On June 28th the 9th Brigade relieved, and the Battalion withdrew to the support line, which coincided with that of the old Black Line of the Battle of Messines. On this day tremendous rains set in, and before long the trenches were filled knee-deep with water, which could not be drained off. The continuous traffic up and down the trenches soon transformed the bottom into a liquid of the consistency of pea-soup, and in that mixture, up to the thighs in many places, the Battalion was destined to live for the next ten days.

Hostile shell fire, now increased greatly in intensity and being accurately directed at the support line and communication trenches, it can be imagined that the life was now no holiday. Practically the whole day was spent in combating the elements in order to procure a dry place to sleep, and at night the carrying parties, with barbed wire, screw pickets, "A" frames, duck-boards, and the dozens of other trench requisites, stumbled and cursed their way up to the destination of their loads.

Morale.

On the evening of July 7th the Battalion again took over the front line. The incessant artillery fire and the awful conditions were now having an effect on the men's nerves, as for a fortnight there had not been the slightest semblance of comfort or safety for the harassed troops. Fritz now became temporarily supreme in the air, and Baron von Richtofen's famous Red Squadron cruising boldly up and down did not add any grains of comfort, as each day saw some gallant British aviator brought down by this outstanding German pilot.

More improvements to the line were carried out here, and strong points were dug by night in front of the main line.

Casualties throughout the whole period had been consistently heavy, and every day throughout the "19 days' stunt," as it was afterwards called, took its toll in the death or mutilation of some well-tried comrade.

The First Hot Meal for Three Weeks.

The Battalion was relieved on July 12th by troops of the 9th Brigade, and whether the relief was known or not to the enemy, the fact remains that the shelling, heavy enough before, increased to the intensity of a barrage over the whole area in which the relief was taking place. On relief the Battalion proceeded to Kemmil, where it received a hot meal and hot tea —practically the first for three weeks—and then a well-earned and much-needed sleep was the rule.

Rum.

Incidents were plentiful, but many will not bear the telling. Rum, as in all stressful periods through-the war, played a prominent part, and was the most cheerfully carried load and the most welcomed issue received by the troops at any time. There is no doubt also that Army rum was "dinkum" rum. One nip warmed the body from head to feet, and in spite of all that has been written to the contrary it did the troops more good than all the prayers of the wowsers who tried to deny it to them.

"It Repeats on Me!"

Sometimes a man was lucky and got more than his share. Sgt. Hourigan (the cook sergeant) on one occasion floundered up to have a look at the front line. He struck the officer of the watch, who asked him if he'd like a nip of rum to keep the cold out. Yes, he would, but when asked if he'd take water with it, he said "No! it's too good to put water in." In any case, there was no room for water, as the cup was full, and Hourigan tossed it off without a pause for breath. Before going away the officer asked him to "have another, Hourigan, you may as well drink it, because I never touch it. It repeats on me!"

Hourigan took it. "Oh, Lord!" he said, raising his eyes, "have mercy on me! Make this repeat on me for ever and ever, Amen." He tossed it off, and feeling that it was a pretty good war after all, ploughed through the mud back to his cookers.

Guy's Luck.

One misty morning Fritz was very daring. In spite of the fact that the trenches at one part of the front were but twenty-five or thirty yards apart, a sniping contest was taking place at anything from 30 to 200 yards distance, and just as one of the 44th boys signalled a "bull," Lieutenant "Alf." Guy, with C.S.M. Dick Cornish, of "A" Company, with more daring than judgment, looked over the top to investigate. The two tin hats at this short distance formed a target which even the worst shot in the German Army could hardly fail to score on, and without a sound the little lieutenant fell to the bottom of the trench, a shot passing through his tin hat and left side of the head. Cornish immediately reported the casualty to the next officer in charge of the line, and an inspection revealed the sad fact that Alf. was apparently "out for keeps." Laying him aside and attending to the at the moment more important business of getting even, the sniping continued, and Sergeant Bert May immediately evened the score by knocking a Fritz's cap (together with a goodly part of his skull) a good three feet in the air. There was no doubt about this Boche going West. However, when matters had quietened down a little, there was another look at Lieut. Guy, chiefly with the object of collecting his little personal belongings to send home, and of performing a hasty trench burial. Before the burial arrangements were complete, however, Alf. showed unmistakable signs of life, and after cancelling the order for burial and amending the casualty report, the officer in charge had him taken out of the trench to the more or less safe precincts of the advanced dressing station, situated about 300 yards from the front line, where the doc. pronounced the little officer had a fighting chance. Removed from there to the security of the clearing station at Steenwerck, he slowly strengthened his very slippery grip on the thread of life, and his strong constitution, coupled with the unremitting care and attention bestowed on him by the doctors of the A.M.C. (in praise of whom enough cannot be said), enabled him to recover and eventually return to W.A. It fell to the lot of few men even in the Great War to have their brains blown on to another man's tin hat and live, but that is exactly what happened in this case. Lieut. Guy is now at Katanning, and only a slight disablement of the leg and arm show traces of his extraordinary ordeal.

Rest on Kemmil Hill.

While at Kemmil the whole of the 11th Brigade was under canvas. The policy was to rest and train the troops; consequently sport figured largely in the programme. In any Brigade competitions the Battalion representatives always upheld the honor of W.A.

THE 19 DAYS' STUNT.

The weather for the first few days was all that could be desired. Later, however, heavy rains tested fully the capabilities of the canvas tents, and found them wanting. Still, comparison with the conditions up the line caused a very philosophic view to be taken of any slight discomforts out of the line. In fact, the reflection which would persist in a man's mind when things were just about as bad as possible that they might be worse kept morale up wonderfully. In the middle of this rainy weather the Battalion was ordered once more to take over the front line.

During the period of the rest on Kemmel Hill, the artillery had been daily increasing its activity, until towards the end of July, as far as the ear and eye could ascertain the whole front was boiling and bubbling with shrapnel and high explosive. The usual trench rumors had it that there was another big attack pending, in which the 11th Brigade was to play an important part.

The Six Days' Stunt.

To the 42nd and 43rd Battalions were allotted the capturing of the objectives on this occasion—a number of enemy outposts near Warneton, the 41st and 44th being given the task of hanging on to the gains when captured. This "hanging on" was a matter of six days, and what with the elements and the artillery, the 44th Diggers who survived look back on it as the worst nightmare of their existence.

On July 29th the Battalion relieved a unit of the 9th Brigade. The rain had converted the trenches into great lengths of muddy drains. Fanny's C.T., the communicatian trench leading up to the line, was knee-deep almost its whole length, and much too deep to be used in quite a number of places. The front line was in no better condition. The action of the water had undermined the walls of the trenches, and every hour saw the destruction of some portion of the parapet or parados which slipped into the trench.

On the morning of July 31st, the attack was duly carried out. On the 11th Brigade front the 42nd and 43rd Battalions were quite successful, and took all their objectives. The 41st and 44th then took over the gains and commenced to "consolidate" and "hang on."

"Hanging On!"

The rain came down in torrents, the shell fire accurately fell on the 44th position in a never ceasing stream of high explosive. This shell-fire increased rather than diminished as the days went on, until it seemed that the only sector worthy of Fritz's attention was that which the 44th Battalion was occupying. The reason for this intensity was that the whole of the attack elsewhere had been a failure, and Fritz was concentrating on the successful sector in order to cause a withdrawal there. Some of the trenches now were absolutely unusable. Sleep was almost an impossibility, owing to the fact that everyone was soaked to the skin the whole time and that nowhere was it possible to lie down. Combine these two factors with a harassing and accurate shell-fire, causing heavy casualties, and possibly the imagination may grasp something of what the 44th Battalion endured during this stunt.

Relief.

On the night of August 3rd, the 16th Battalion relieved the 44th, and the relief with which the latter marched out was tempered with sympathy for the poor devils who had just marched in. The 16th Battalion was raided two hours after it took over the trenches. Even now the 44th's troubles were not over. Shell-fire seemed to follow them all the way out, and it was not until the old front line in front of Messines was reached that they reckoned they were safe.

Thus ended the 44th's part in the Battle of Messines and subsequent operations connected with that battle. The survivors, few in numbers and shaken in morale, laid themselves down that night in their coating of mud in the welcome shelter of the huts of Aldershot Camp, near Neuve Eglise, and thought that the best way to end this war and prevent future wars would be to put those charged with its responsibility into the hell from which they had just emerged. Certain it is that a ballot would then result in submitting the dispute to arbitration.

CHAPTER XI.

THE BATTLE OF BROODSEINDE RIDGE.

"Old Bill's" Thousand.

The 44th had been badly battered in the Messines fighting, and "Old Bill's" Thousand was now but a shadow of the lusty fighting force which had left Fremantle just a short year before. Many old faces were missing from the depleted ranks, but in their passing they had established glorious precedents which set a high standard for the new arrival, and which to their credit be it said, the reinforcements never lowered.

Col. Mansbridge was now posted to staff duties in England, and the sense of loss to the Battalion in parting with "Old Bill," the individual who had guided its destinies from its "toddling" days until it had fully matured as a fighting unit, was very great indeed. Lieut.-Col. J. P. Clark, a Tasmanian officer from the 40th Battalion, now took command of the 44th.

The Value of Sport Recognised.

After a few days' rest the Battalion marched to Waterlands Camp, near Nieppe, and the 11th Brigade took over the duties of reserve to the 51st (British) Division, occupying the Armentieres sector. Here two new factors made their appearance. The first was the sudden and definite recognition of sport as a necessary factor in the training of a soldier for active service. This meant that the mornings now consisted of the ordinary military training, but the

A GERMAN MACHINE GUN POST NEAR ZONNEBEKE.

This was a concrete dug-out built into the ruins of a farm. The occupants fought to a finish! Note the thickness of the concrete.

THE TERRIFIC WASTAGE OF WAR.

A corduroy road which drew its full share of "crabs" in the attacks on Paschendale. Such pictures as this one give the civilian a far better idea of the word "desolation" than columns of description.

afternoons were given over entirely to sports of all kinds. As the weather was decent, and with no other distractions, the sporting events were entered into with all the vim and vigor which characterised the Digger, and this resulted after the first fortnight in an appreciable decrease in the number on sick parades.

Gothas!

The second factor was the introduction of organised bombing raids on a large scale over the areas occupied by troops behind the line. Almost every night the bombing squadrons of both combatants did their best to make sleep impossible, and the sentry's three whistle blasts (for lights out) were always promptly obeyed.

The immensity of the air organisation now could be seen even by the infantryman. By day the lines of observation balloons, the aeroplanes, scouting and fighting, and the anti-aircraft guns on motor lorries were very much in evidence. By night the bombing planes, the dozens of searchlights crisscrossing across the heavens and seeking to get the intruders inside their rays, and the thunder of the anti-aircraft guns' barrage on to some located 'plane —these, with the extra "windy" feeling which all in the affected area felt when bombs were falling from space, left no possible doubt as to the part the air was playing in this war.

The aforesaid bombing 'planes created more fear at night than the actual damage they caused deserved, and on the rare occasions when one was brought down, either by a lucky "Archie" hit or by the tracer bullet of a British fighting 'plane, there was genuine, triumphant, and excusable exultation at the sight of the blazing bomber falling to earth, where generally its bombs burst on impact, and completed the jig-saw puzzle.

Under these conditions time was passed up to August 20, when the Battalion left the battle sphere for the back areas, to reorganise, refit, and train for further big work which lay ahead.

Merck.

Entraining at Steenwerck station, after the usual discomforts of a troop train, the Battalion detrained at Wizernes, and then a fourteen kilometre march brought them to Merck St. Lievin, the prettiest little village that it was ever the 44th's luck to strike in France. Situated in a deep valley, through which a small river flowed, with fruit trees and crops surrounding it, a general air of prosperity, and no signs of war, excepting the absence of the men-folk, Merck gave promise of a very enjoyable time. The village people had had no troops billeted on them for two years, and were inclined to look sideways at the Australians at first, in consequence of the characteristics which rumor had credited them with. However, the Digger soon fixed that, and before two days had gone by he was a part and parcel of Merck, playing with the kiddies and helping with the farm work, as if he'd been there for years.

St. Pierre.

As bad luck would have it, the Battalion was only allowed one week at Merck, because at this stage the necessity for it as an artillery area was recognised. The 44th then moved to an area around St. Pierre, where, as the villages were small, the companies were scattered over a very wide area. Headquarters and "D" Company were at St. Pierre, "A" Company at Salveque, "B" at Cantemerle, and "C" at Fourdebecque.

BATTLE OF BROODSEINDE RIDGE.

Preparations were now in hand for another big attack, and morning and afternoon found all hands fitting themselves for their various jobs. Sport was still a big factor and helped to build the stamina of the troops up to a very high standard; and if ever stamina was needed, it was to be needed in the next stunt, as the 44th found to its cost. On September 25, the march was begun back to the battle area, and three stiff marches brought the Battalion to Poperinghe, where they camped in tents just outside the town. For the first time during the war the five Australian Divisions were in the same area. Two were already in the thick of the fighting in front of Ypres, and the other three were soon to be thrown into it, literally "up to the neck."

Poperinghe was the railhead for the British troops fighting in the Ypres salient, and as the fighting on the Western Front was now practically confined to this sector, it became a target for aerial bombing raids on a tremendous scale. While the 44th was under canvas here their sleep and rest was disturbed every night by these raids, and although no actual casualties were incurred, one small bomb fell in the middle of the cricket pitch, and another very close to some tents.

The Air Raids.

The difference in sound of British and German 'planes was marked. The former's engines made a level purr, while the latter buzzed loud and soft alternately. Each bomber carried five big bombs, each about 3 feet 6 inches long and a foot in diameter. The "windy" feeling was felt by everyone, although not everyone would admit it. With all hands sound asleep in a tent, comes the unmistakeable buzz of the Bosche. Boom! one! Boom! two (nearer); Boom!

three (still closer but half a mile away yet). Not a sound or a move from the "sleepers." Boom! four (seemingly in the next field). A slight uneasy stir. Boom! the fifth and last. A simultaneous and deep sigh of relief from everyone, a general turning over and wriggling and twisting, and the occupants settle down once more to their interrupted slumber. And slumber, too, that might have been their last if the luck had varied ever so little.

There was a Chinese compound near the camp and the yellow men were terrified at these Gothas. Every night as the first one came over they would pick up their belongings and scatter in chattering groups all over the countryside.

The 28th Battalion was camped close by at this period and, not so lucky as the 44th, one bomb practically wiped out all its senior officers. Another, which fell on a tent occupied by the 11th Australian M.G. Coy., killed and wounded 60 men—nearly a quarter of the strength of the company.

Reconnaissance of the front area by officers and n.c.o.'s was now the rule. The front was not too stable and these parties could not get much definite knowledge as to where the front line actually was; still each party got a general knowledge of conditions and the area in which they had to move later, and this considerably helped the subsequent operations.

The Nucleus.

On October 2nd, a portion of the nucleus (a percentage of all ranks was kept out of fights so that no matter how heavy the losses were the Battalion would have a nucleus of old hands to graft the reinforcements on to) was sent up to do a cable-bury. They travelled in 'buses and had no sooner alighted when a Fritz aeroplane dropped bombs and killed and wounded about twenty men.

Ypres.

On October 3rd the 44th Battalion, 700 strong, fit and full of fight and confidence, moved from Poperinghe along the Ypres road, through Ypres past the ruins of the famous Cloth Hall, past Hell Fire Corner and into the Menin Road. The Menin Road was even then littered with dead horses, wrecked motor 'buses, smashed railway trucks, and every conceivable item of the terrific wastage of war. Off the Menin Road the 44th bivouaced in a field, having lunch and resting while final arrangements were made for the attack on Broodseinde Ridge next morning.

The Approach March.

At 10 p.m. that night the Battalion commenced its approach march, and moved in single file to its assembly position on Hill 40 near Zonnebeke, across five miles of shell-torn ground. The Zonnebeke was ordinarily a small creek, but shell-fire had so chopped and churned it up that it formed an impassable liquid morass about 150 yards across.

The Assembly at Zonnebeke.

When the head of the column (and 700 men in single file on a dark night form "some" column) reached the Zonnebeke it was found that the duckboard bridge over it had just been shot away. There was nothing for it but to sit the Battalion in their tracks while the guide found another crossing. After an hour's search in the darkness and mud, another bridge was found closer to the railway line, and by 2 a.m. on October 4 the whole Battalion was assembled in its allotted position. This approach march was a difficult operation in itself, as owing to the lack of opportunities for thorough reconnaissance it was necessary that the Battalion should be led by the one guide, and as all A.I.F. men are aware, the job of suiting the pace at the head of the column to the requirements of the men towards its rear was no easy one. However, the pace set was no more than one mile per hour, and touch was maintained and without any disorganisation, and with only a few casualties by shell fire the assembly was completed.

The Australian attack was timed to start at 6 a.m., and their barrage was to come down a few minutes before that. During the preceding hours the Aussie guns were very quiet.

The Iron Division.

As it happened Fritz had decided to attack the Australian positions on the same morning (October 4), but he was 10 minutes too late, as his attack was timed to commence at 6.10 a.m. His troops, among whom were the famous Iron Division, which was noted as never having lost a trench or failed to take its objective, were assembling at the same time as the Australians, and when both had completed their arrangements there were, unknown to each other, two bodies of assault troops lying in some places with only fifty yards between them, and both waiting for the dawn to fly at each other's throats.

The German Barrage.

As the Australian guns were practically silent, the German troops on their assembly positions must have had a quiet time. Not so the Diggers. The German barrage started at 3 a.m. and from that time up to 6 o'clock the troops endured an ever-increasing storm of high explosive shells, which literally showered on the area in which the Diggers were crouching in shell holes, with no possible cover and only waiting the arrival of the "one" which must sooner or later fall in their particular shell hole. Casualties in the 44th were numerous. "D" Company lost fifty per cent. of its strength in those three hours, and the other companies also suffered heavily. In addition, the usual Flanders drizzle drenched everyone to the skin. Although under such circumstances the wetting was of minor importance, it was still another of those proverbial straws which, however, never broke the Diggers' backs. Only those who endured it can now imagine what the suspense was like.

The Attack on Broodseinde Ridge.

Suddenly a flash of fire behind and a thunderous, deafening roar in front gave notice that the Australian guns were hitting back. Then as the barrage went forward, the infantry, eager for action, followed it closely, and dead, wounded and dazed Germans met the view everywhere. The enemy attack was completely dislocated, and five minutes from the opening of the barrage his attacking troops were either casualties or on their way back as prisoners of war. However, isolated concrete dug-outs, protected from shell fire and manned by staunch machine gunners, held out, and each of these caused many casualties before they were wiped out. These survivors did not hold up the general advance, and the spectacle then was lines of casual Australians following the barrage with rifles slung, smoking cigarettes or "souvenired" cigars. If a machine-gun opened there was a converging rush on to it. A machine-gun post was always good for a few first-class revolvers and various pairs of field-glasses. Under these "picnic" conditions the advance went on, and, "according to plan" by 10 a.m. Broodseinde Ridge was taken and was being consolidated by the 41st

Battalion, with the 44th three hundred yards in rear as supports.

Enemy artillery at first was non-existent, having been completely silenced by the Australian counter-battery fire, but as these guns ceased fire and moved forward, so the Hun fire increased.

The Dead on the Railway Lines.

The German casualties were extraordinarily heavy. The Zonnebeke-Passchendale railway line was literally heaped with dead, where the awful artillery fire must have caught them packed for their own attack. Broodseinde Ridge and the area around Zonnebeke was also littered with bodies.

The average depth of the advance was 2400 yards. The Third Division alone took over 2000 German prisoners, so that the enemy's total losses on the whole front must have been enormous.

The weather up to this time had been fair,, and the drizzles which had fallen had not been enough to make the ground muddy.

On October 5 two enemy counter-attacks took place, but they were broken by the Australian artillery before the infantry had a chance with the rifle.

Relief.

On the evening of October 6 the 44th were relieved by a Battalion of the 66th Manchesters. Rain fell heavily during the day, and, unfortunately, the Manchesters made their approach march with full packs, an error of judgment on someone's part which eventually caused many deaths from exhaustion in the sea of mud that the area became within the next few days.

VILLERS BRETONNEAUX CHURCH.
August, 1918.

HAMEL.

BATTLE OF BROODSEINDE RIDGE.

The 44th now moved back to Eerie Camp, a mile or so behind Ypres, there to rest and reorganise for another "hop-over."

Casualties.

The losses in the three days of Broodseinde fighting had been four officers and 60 men killed, with about 250 all ranks wounded, most of which were sustained in the bombardment prior to the assault. The C.O., Lieut.-Colonel Clark, and the adjutant, Capt. Hillary, had both been wounded on the first morning, and the command of the Battalion had fallen on to the capable shoulders of Major M. H. A'Beckett.

A popular officer in Capt. Tom Bone, of "A" Coy., was killed by a shell on the Broodseinde Ridge. In addition to being a brave and efficient soldier, Tom had a beautiful voice, and his singing at the various camp concerts had always been keenly appreciated by all who heard him.

Lieut. Pitman, who was awarded the M.C. at Messines, was also killed, and left a place as signalling officer which it was very hard to fill.

HAMEL.

(See photo on previous page.)

Capt. Moran, of the 43rd Battalion (which was entrusted with the task of "mopping up" Hamel village), made a bet before the action that he would fly the flag of France that day over Hamel. He nailed it to the ridge pole of the highest house.

CHAPTER XII.

PASCHENDALE!

The rain now fell heavily and incessantly. Owing to the heavy casualties at Broodseinde, the Battalion had now to modify its organisation, and companies were reduced to three platoons instead of the original four. On the morning of October 9, they moved from Eerie Camp to bivouac for the night on Freezenberg Ridge. The road from Poperinghe to Ypres is a great wide highway, lined with noble trees on each side, and it was the main artery serving the British troops in the Ypres salient. Night and day it was crammed with transport and troops, both going and coming, and the fact that there were no serious blocks reflects credit on the traffic control organisation. A block for any length of time would have meant miles and miles of hopeless confusion. The Battalion could only move here in single file and right on the edge of the road.

Freezenberg Ridge was reached towards evening, and the men made shelters in the old trenches abounding in the vicinity.

The Manchesters' Attack.

At dawn on the 10th, the 66th Manchesters launched an attack on Paschendale. The attack was a hopeless failure—doomed at the start by the fact that the men carried packs. (Australian troops always went into action in "fighting order," i.e., no pack or greatcoat.) The rain still coming down in torrents had turned the whole battle area into a sea of churned-up mud. It was bad enough moving light, but to be burdened with a pack made it impossible for any man to do a fighting man's job. The Manchesters failed where no troops in the world under the same conditions would have succeeded.

Through the Barrage!

As a result of this failure the 11th Brigade was ordered on the afternoon of the 10th to regain and hold the front line of the day before. The whole Brigade moved off in artillery formation of platoons, breaking down to sections. Soon after the advance was begun, however, a German 'plane flew over and evidently wirelessed the information back to the guns, because soon afterwards it seemed that every gun on the Western Front was dropping its shells on to, and in front of the 11th Brigade. Darkness was now coming on and crossing Hill 40 and descending into the valley of death beyond was an experience of which no pen can adequately describe the horrors. The mud was knee-deep, and barbed wire was strewn around in hopeless confusion. The 44th at this stage was split up into little groups struggling and cursing their way forward, many men being killed and wounded, and the survivors exhausted and covered with mud. Before the position was reached darkness fell, with no abatement of the extraordinary shell-fire. Organised movement had long been impossible, and it stands as a monument to the Digger that not one man turned back. Despite the sheer horror of the whole operation, when morning dawned the 44th Battalion was lying in the mud on a line approximating that which they had taken on October 4, and from which the Manchesters had moved into their attack on Paschendale the morning before. There were isolated gaps in the line and the whole day was spent in filling these, securing intelligence, sending back reports, and generally "getting the hang" of the whole show.

Sniping and the White Flag.

Enemy sniping was very keen, and Fritz in the early morning was quite confident and incautious. Lieut. "Jock" Drummond, of the 44th, was shot through the head by one of these snipers, and, as he was an exceedingly popular officer, his death caused every man in the Battalion to become a sniper thirsting for revenge. The result was that by the afternoon, superiority of fire was established. It was impossible for a German to show himself without becoming the target for several rifles, and his casualties from sniping alone were so severe that he sent several stretcher parties out under a white flag to attend to them.

"Stretcher Bearer!"

Seizing this opportunity the 44th stretcher-bearers went forward and brought in numbers of Manchester men, wounded in the previous day's fight. This was the only occasion in the 44th's existence that friend and foe worked alongside each other without molestation.

Before dusk a severe bombardment was opened on the back areas. All important dug-outs likely to be used as headquarters, the artillery positions, and roads and tracks were heavily and accurately peppered with all sizes and descriptions of shells. The position along the front line remained the same that night. It still rained off and on, and the carrying and ration parties, stetcher-bearers and runners—in fact anyone whose job was a moving one—had an almost intolerable time. The so-called tracks were almost impassable and the wounded had to be man-handled in relays for a distance of anything up to five miles to a dressing station.

The Men with Moving Jobs.

The ration parties—each man with two sandbags full of rations, and the carrying parties with their loads of duckboards, ammunition, etc.—came up each night, and their devotion to duty and the high standard of "dinkum" discipline which they had attained alone made it possible for the front line troops to "hang on." The system of control of the scattered units of the Battalion was by messages delivered by runner. By day and night these runners kept up communication, and the initiative and "nouse" displayed at night in finding the individuals to whom the messages were addressed formed another link in the long chain of testimony to the individuality shown by the Aussie soldier.

At 4 a.m. on October 12, the Battalion was relieved by a unit of the 10th Brigade, which, in conjunction with the 9th Brigade, the 4th Australian Division on the right and the New Zealanders on the left, was to make another attempt that morning to gain possession of the coveted village of Paschendale and the ridge upon which it stood.

On relief the 44th moved back in the darkness and took up a position on Hill 40, near Zonnebeke. It still rained, and the physical condition of the men now was very bad. The continuous soaking for days had caused trench feet to become prevalent, and many good men, utterly unable to walk and with legs swollen to twice their natural size, had to be evacuated for this reason. Many more developed pneumonia, which took them in a very bad form.

Mustard Gas.

Fritz had been using a mustard-gas shell consistently through the Paschendale fighting, and this form of gas poisoning was awful in its effect. One whiff would send a man to hospital a choking, spluttering wreck, and even sitting in the mud where one had burst hours before resulted in tremendous blisters and burns all over the body. Under these conditions of exposure to the elements at their worst, wet clothing, gas, and fatigue, it can be understood that every man was suffering the torments of hell on earth.

Unknown British Soldiers.

Near the position at Zonnebeke which the 44th now occupied, British troops from all parts of the world had been fighting heavily for the past three months, with no appreciable gain in territory for their tremendous efforts. The dead in most places could not be buried, and they lay in the mud until they disappeared from sight. In one shell hole alone were seen five dead men, evidently killed on various dates—an English officer, a colored King's African Rifleman, a New Zealander, a Highlander, and an Australian. The latter was apparently the last to occupy the crater, and he met his death with his Lewis gun to his shoulder. Such a "grave" in itself lent a grim significance to the term World War, for the bugle call had brought these willing fighters together from every British corner of it. In life strangers; in death comrades united.

Paschendale Entered.

The attack on the 12th had no better success than that of the 10th. In this case Paschendale was actually entered by troops of the 10th Brigade, but the New Zealanders on the left were held up by absolutely impassible well-wired swamps, commanded by shell-proof concrete block-houses and manned by determined German machine gunners. As a result of this left flank hold-up, the 9th and 10th Brigades came under heavy rifle and machine gun fire from the flank, which cut them to pieces, disorganised them, and caused both Brigades to take the best cover they could. It was not until late in the day, however, when it was found that the New Zealanders could not clear the flank, that the troops came back—and the coming back was a worse operation than the going forward. As a result of this failure the 9th and 10th Brigades were weakened in numbers to such an extent that the 11th Brigade had to move forward and occupy a front line once more as near as possible to the line gained on October 4. Think of it! Since October 4 two big battles—one on October 10, by English troops, and the other on October 12, by Australians and New Zealanders—had been fought without advancing the line a single yard. The enemy artillery fire was certainly very heavy, and his machine gunners good, but what killed both attacks as it had killed others was M-U-D.

The 44th, after the gruelling they had been getting from October 4 onwards, were by no means fit for the task on hand. The Germans, having repulsed two attacks, were confident. Their artillery fire was much heavier than the Australian, probably owing to the fact that the latter's percentage of artillery casualties had been extraordinary owing to their immobility caused by the mud, which restricted their movements to the few roads in the area and prevented all attempts to get positions off them. The enemy artillery on the other hand was not so handicapped by immobility, as they were in action on ground which had not been consistently ploughed up by shell fire for years, as the territory had been in which the Australians were then located.

"Hold the Line!"

Here commenced another trying period in the history of the Battalion. It had entered the fighting on October 4 with seven hundred men. These were now reduced to three hundred, all more or less physically unfit for the strenuous task which lay ahead. This task of holding the line was for an indefinite period, and as the 9th and 10th Brigades had been withdrawn from the fight altogether, it was hopeless to look for relief to them. The next ten days was a continuous nightmare. Two Battalions of the Brigade were in the front line, and two occupied the support positions which were along Hill 40 and about a mile behind the front line. The Battalions took turns at this, and it was hard to say which was the better position—front line or support, both were so bad. It still rained. In fact, from the 7th to 21st October it hardly stopped. Dry clothing and boots were unknown. Boots —Australian, and the best issued to any troops fighting—were like wet sponges, and every step was handicapped by the pounds of mud which clung to them. Enemy artillery was never more vindictive. Night and day his shells, gas and high explosive, searched out every nook and corner which it was possible for troops to occupy. Casualties were heavy and the evacuations from trench feet and pneumonia made the task of the few survivors even more arduous than it would otherwise have been. About October 15th some two hundred and fifty reinforcements, fresh from England, joined the Battalion, and their first experience of active service was an exceptionally hard one.

Relief!

On the night of October 21 one company of Canadians relieved the worn-out 44th Battalion on Hill 40. A tired and broken remnant straggled out of that

PEAR TRENCH.
The enemy occupying Pear Trench put up a stout resistance, and hung up the advance in front of Hamel for a short period. Their fight was to a finish!

CHARLIE COMBEN LEWIS GUNNER IN "B" COY.
Killed in Action 4/7/18.

"YAK."
Sgt. J. E. V. K. Ingvarsen, D.C.M., who was recommended for the V.C. in the last stunt.

hellish battlefield of Paschendale, 8 officers and 150 men in number—all that was left of 42 officers and 950 men who had been engaged in it for various periods from October 4th to 21st. For eighteen days they had struggled incessantly against the Hun and the elements, and the effects of that struggle were felt by the survivors for many a long day afterwards.

The Opinion of the Digger on Paschendale.

The general opinion of the Diggers on the Paschendale fighting was that it was a tragic blunder, and that had the authorities realised by personal reconnaissance what a morass the whole battle area was turned into by October 9, the operations would have ceased. As it turned out, the Canadians, fresh and fit, took another five weeks, and a series of strenuous operations, which caused them very severe losses, before they finally took Paschendale. By that time the whole British Army was exhausted. The occupation of Paschendale did not cause the Germans to fall back on the flanks, and simply resulted in the creation of a British salient in which the trenches were subject to artillery fire from the front and both flanks.

Individuals.

For individuals in the Paschendale fighting, as at Messines, the hat goes off to the stretcher-bearers. It is safe to assert that never, since man made war, could the carriage of the wounded from the field of battle to the dressing station have been accomplished under worse conditions than prevailed during October 1917. The 44th stretcher-bearers did all that mortal men could do. Not only did they evacuate all their own wounded, but scores of 66th Manchesters, 9th and 10th Brigade Australians, and many Germans were carried by them across that field of death; and to take one wounded man from the firing line to the dressing stations was a four-man job for twelve, fourteen and even twenty-four hours.

Private Cook, Superman!

Private Cook, M.M., was a super-man. From October 4 to the 23rd he labored like a giant. His mates were killed; the casuality he was carrying on one occasion was killed, but Cook was untouched. After the Manchesters failed, Cook it was who went first in front of the outposts on his errand of mercy. Practically without a spell he worked day and night, and finally, when the remnants of the Battalion were relieved, he approached the adjutant and requested to be allowed to stay in with the Canadians, as there were still casualties not yet brought in. He was not ordered to come out, and so stayed in, and two days later had his shoulder smashed by shell fire. He was recommended for the V.C.; and surely if ever man earned one in this great war, that man was Private Cook. He did not even receive a bar to the Military Medal which he had previously won. Such inconsistencies in the bestowal of decorations frequently made the blood of the Diggers boil.

Lieutenant "Joe" Rogers was detailed to stay with the nucleus for the October 4 operation on Broodseinde. He "bought" himself a job, however, in command of some anti-aircraft Lewis gunners, and "hopped the bags" with the rest of the Battalion. Near the objective he mounted his guns, and on the second day, a five-nine landed in among them, killing some and wounding most. Joe bandaged the wounded, and saw every one evacuated, was bandaged himself but stayed on with the remnants of his crews. Relieved on the 6th, he marched out, and while waiting for motor-lorries in Ypres was busy writing a casuality report when the adjutant noticed his bandages. There was a big hole in his neck, and he was bandaged practically from head to foot, yet had not even reported himself a casualty. When ordered into an ambulance, he was the most down-hearted man who ever left the Battalion. In hospital afterwards he underwent no less than thirteen operations to extract the pieces of shell with which he was splattered. Such was the spirit of the A.I.F.!

Decorations.

Many decorations were awarded, but still many more were earned without receiving official recognition. Major A'Beckett was awarded the D.S.O., Captain Bremner and Lieutenant Roy Maddeford the M.C. Lieutenant Maddeford belonged to "A" Company, and was the only officer of the company left in both the Broodseinde stunt and the subsequent long-drawn-out occupation of the line. This made the third occasion on which the officer commanding "A" Company had been killed and all the others rendered casualties with the exception of one.

On October 22, the remnants moved back per motor-'bus to St. Pierre, to the billets which they had left less than four weeks before, and to which but a very small percentage returned.

CHAPTER XIII.

THE BREAK THROUGH.

Building Up.

The Battalion remained in the St. Pierre vicinity for about a month. It was recognised that the troops needed a decent spell in order to allow them to regain morale, which had been badly shattered in the Paschendale fighting. Parades were therefore easy; concerts were organised and took place two or three times per week; football matches were played between companies and other Battalions, and Brigade, and Divisional sports meetings were arranged. Leave was fairly liberal, both to Paris and Blighty, and every possible effort was made for the time being to thrust war and all the horrors it meant to the fighting men into the background. Reinforcements joined up, both officers and men, but it was noticeable at this period that the majority of these reinforcements were either the sick or wounded who had returned from hospital.

With the Battalion up to a strength of about 450 all ranks, a move back to the line was made about the middle of November. On this occasion the 11th Brigade was in reserve to the 9th and 10th, and merely occupied camps in rear of the line. Training here was entered into thoroughly—with physical training in the forefront. Games were organised on a more extensive scale than ever before, and during the afternoons, without exception, every man took an active part in either a game of football, hockey, or mobbing. The last-named was the best of all games to achieve the result aimed at.

Mobbing.

This game took place on any old ground—even a ploughed field became level after one or two games—with goal posts at each end; a leather or hessian bag filled with straw, and equal numbers of men, from twenty to forty on each side. There were no rules, excepting that the "ball" must not be kicked, and the object was to force or throw it through the opposing side's goal posts. It was strenuous, easily learnt, and caused great excitement between companies and platoons. This simple game, on account of the fact that everyone could play it, and once playing, was infected with the spirit of it, was responsible for the Battalion attaining a very high standard of physical fitness.

Le Bizet.

After moving from one camp to another in the Kemmel district until December, with nothing especially exciting to break the monotony, the Battalion took over the front line at Le Bizet, near Plugstreet Wood, a quiet sector with the river Lys flowing in between the two front lines. This was the quietest period of front line duty enjoyed by the 44th, and except for patrol encounters, nothing much happened to show that there was a war on. Fritz's line was close to the river, while the 44th's was three hundred yards from the bank. In that area of No Man's Land were several ruined buildings, and around these every night crept the patrols of both sides.

Patrol Encounters!

On two occasions patrol encounters took place. On the first in which a patrol under the command of Lieut. Stevens encountered a big party of Germans in No Man's Land, the enemy retreated in disorder, leaving one dead and one prisoner. On the second, the 44th lost a popular little officer in Lieut. Joe Crawley, who was seized by hidden Bosch, and, struggling and fighting, was shot through the head. The rest of the 44th patrol then coming up, the Huns made off and the body was brought in. The most unfortunate part of the affair was that Lieut. Crawley had been detailed to proceed to England in two days' time for six months' duty in a training camp. He was not ordered to go out on this particular patrol (which was under the command of the scout officer), but because some of his own platoon were going out, he elected to go with them, as he said "for the last time." The pathetic truth of the words!

Rumors.

This was in December, and although on no part of the Western front was much doing in the way of active warfare, all sorts of rumors were rife; and the newspapers were full of details of the great German offensive which was to be launched in the spring.

January and February were spent in a similar manner to December. In the line, in billets, and in camp. Training was quietly carried on. Games, sports, and concerts occupied all spare time. The ranks were refilled, and at the beginning of March 1918, the 3rd Division left the Belgian front line area, as it turned out, to see its blood-stained swamps no more, and went back to a rest area near Boulogne, where the 44th Battalion was billetted in the village of Lottinghem.

Platoon Training.

In Lottinghem special attention was paid to musketry and Lewis gun training. The platoon organisation at this time consisted of a Lewis gun section, rifle grenade section, bombing section, and a section of riflemen. With these four, each with its own special weapon, it was possible for a platoon commander to organise little schemes for the platoon in attack, which would bring out the characteristics of each weapon. These schemes were most interesting, and with a platoon commander who knew what he wanted, and who had the knack of imparting his knowledge and allowed a "sit easy and smoke" argument by the whole platoon afterwards, the maximum amount of benefit was obtained by all concerned.

Ordered South!

Rumors of the coming Hun offensive were now very prevalent, but exactly on what part of the front it was to fall no one knew. On March 21 it materialised on the 5th Army front down South. That it was a serious break-through was proved by the fact that throughout the British Forces in France all leave was stopped, schools cancelled, and officers recalled to units. On March 23, the 3rd Division was ordered South, and the 44th left Lottinghem on that day and marched to Arques, where they billetted for the night. Next morning they entrained for the Somme.

The Somme!

The next three days and nights were a succession of railway journeys, route marches, and 'bus rides, about which no one who took part can have more than a confused recollection, and at the end of which, 5 p.m. on March 27, found the Battalion assembled with some troops of the 9th and 10th Brigades in a valley just outside the little village of Heilly. Isolated shells were falling on the ridges in the vicinity. The civilian population, with the exception of a few old men and women, had evacuated their homes, and the whole countryside was deserted. At 6 p.m. company commanders were called to Battalion headquarters and were issued with their battle instructions. Companies at this time were up to strength and were close on 200 strong. "D" Company was sent up to form a front line near Sailly-le-Sec, under the orders of the C.O. 42nd Battalion. "B" Company was ordered to occupy Corbie, an important town on the junction of the Ancre and Somme Rivers, with instructions to hold to the last man the bridges across the river. "A" and "C" Companies were sent to occupy villages along the Ancre. No information was available for company commanders to work on as to where the enemy was supposed to be. The only maps available were small scale road maps, and of these only one per company. The country was strange, as it was the first time the Third Division had been in the Somme area, and in addition the night was dark.

At 7 p.m. companies moved off under advance guards, after a short explanation to the men by company commanders, giving all the information available and pointing out that the 44th was up against it, and the only thing to do was for every individual to take what was coming to him and to give of his best.

Each company got into its correct position before morning. The Hun was not encountered. South-East of Corbie, English cavalry went through and reconnoitred before dawn towards Villers Brettonneaux, returning with a few prisoners and the report that enemy patrols were active in that direction.

SOME OF THE BATTALION S.B.'s.

THE OLD PLATOON.

Before marching to their assembly positions prior to a stunt, the platoons were generally given a few final instructions by their commanders. This is a typical turnout on such an occasion.

THE BREAK THROUGH.   125

The next day, March 25, troops of the 9th Brigade took over the 44th positions on the Somme, and "A," "B," and "C" Companies were ordered to assemble at a brickworks on the high ground north of the Somme. They assembled about 4 p.m., and received fresh orders for an attack that night, the 44th's part of which was to be the village of Sailly Laurette, held by the Germans.

The most exciting incident which happened while the companies were waiting there occurred when L/C. Vaudrey was juggling with three bombs in the air at once. One fell to the ground, and the next coming down hit it and knocked the pin out. There was a scatter and a yell, and Vaudrey, diving on the bomb, threw it blindly as far as he could. It landed alongside three officers who were lying under a bush studying their map. They lay flat, and it burst without doing them any injury. It caused one casualty, however, as Pte. Luff received a piece in the calf of the leg. The most pleased man over the whole performance was the same Luff.

Sailly-le-Sec.

The orders were to the effect that if stiff resistance was encountered, the troops were to dig in west of Sailly Laurette. If the opposition was only slight, then they were to go right through and consolidate on a certain line east of that village. The three companies were issued with one bomb per man, and "A" and "C" Companies with picks and shovels. "B" Company was to support the attack but was not issued with either picks or shovels, as there was a shortage of these very necessary fighting man's tools. The advance commenced towards evening in artillery formation of platoons. Down valleys, up steep hillsides, which caused much fatigue. The night turned very dark and a drizzly rain fell. The approach was over ground totally unknown to the troops participating, and all the information about it, unbelievable as it sounds, had been gleaned by the officers from the one solitary road map issued per company. At 9.30 p.m., the line of outposts formed by the 42nd Battalion, in front of Sailly-le-Sec was passed through. At this time all hands were wearing oilsheets over their shoulders on account of the rain. "A" and "C" Companies were extended with the right flank of "C" Company resting on the Somme River and the left of "A" Company in touch with the 41st Battalion, advancing on the left. "B" Company was still in artillery formation about 300 yards in rear.

At 10 p.m., from Sailly Laurette cemetery a German flare went up. The light glistened on the line of wet oil sheets. Sharp commands rapped out, and a storm of machine gun bullets swept through the luckless members of "A" and "C" Companies. There was absolutely no cover, the ground being perfectly flat, with not even a friendly shell hole. Orders had been given that rifle-fire was not to be resorted to, consequently the men lay down where they were, and vainly tried to scoop a few shovelfuls of earth together to form some sort of protection against the merciless hail of lead. Flare after flare went up. No Huns could be seen, but the sharp commands of their officers could be plainly heard. Captain Rockliffe, of "C" Company, who was in charge of the assault, moved along taking stock of the situation, and he then decided to withdraw the line about 100 yards to a more favorable position and dig in. By this time the two companies had had about thirty men killed and sixty wounded, and what with the darkness and the fact that the ground had never been seen in daylight,

THE BREAK THROUGH.

there was an understandable degree of confusion. It was war at its worst.

Digging In!

Notwithstanding all these difficulties, however, the withdrawal to the fresh position was carried out, all the wounded and many of the dead being brought back also. One platoon from each company then dug in while the remaining platoons withdrew to a valley outside Sailly-le-Sec.

Two popular officers killed in this operation were Lieut. Stevens (Stevie) of "A" Company and Lieut. Bob Casey of "C" Company. Many of the Diggers next morning found that their equipment and clothing had been pierced through and through by bullets.

"B" Company, while these stirring events were taking place, had taken up a position on the shoulder of a hill overlooking Sailly Laurette, in some old French trenches dug to a depth of about three feet. They put in the night by improving these positions as much as possible, and obtaining touch and information from the troops on the flanks. Until daylight came, however, no one knew exactly their own whereabouts or that of the enemy. When dawn did arrive, Fritz's outposts could be seen in Sailly Laurette cemetery, and as there appeared no immediate danger of an attack the tired troops, with a sentry over each group, lay down in their shallow holes and snatched some well-earned sleep. During the day orders were received that "B" Company would relieve the two platoons of "A" and "C" Companies in the evening and then remain as an outpost company, protecting the front of, and under the orders of, the 42nd Battalion.

"On to Amiens!"

On this day, March 29, from the position of the two platoons left occupying the hill, great activity was noticed in the Hun territory south-east of Sailly Laurette. Motor 'buses full of troops, transport, and marching infantry, showed plainly that they intended to renew their "On to Amiens!" advance at an early date. With the relief of "A" and "C" Companies' platoons, "B" Company now became responsible for a front of over 2000 yards from the Somme River northwards, with an enemy attack obviously imminent. The night was spent in preparing for it, and there was never any doubt in "B" Coy's collective mind as to the reception they would give the attackers when they came. At dawn, although advised by Brigade headquarters that Fritz would attack at that hour, nothing happened, and the company settled down to rest, with watchful sentries over each section of trench.

"Coming Over!"

At 12 noon on March 30 the cry came, "Fritz is coming over!"—and coming he was. From Sailly Laurette, they advanced in a body, for all the world like a huge crowd just dispersing on the completion of a football match in the village. They had congregated in the houses during the night, and at their zero hour they burst forth practically in one vast crowd. On the south side of the Somme, and also north of Sailly Laurette, where the ground was open, the attackers advanced in long lines, one following the other at about 100 yards distance. A storm of bullets from a machine gun barrage swept "B" Company's trenches, but had no effect in its object of keeping down the heads and fire of the defenders. The company was not long getting going. A few isolated cracks, and then a rattle and a roar of Lewis

THE BREAK THROUGH. 129

gun, machine gun and rifle fire. Lewis gunners, with coats off and one boot on, just roused from sleep, were using their weapons with splendid effect. Rifles became hot, but the fire never slackened. In ten minutes' time the Hun attack was completely demoralised, and in less than half an hour he was driven to earth and shelter—by the rifle and Lewis gun fire of one company of 180 men over a front of 2000 yards! There was no doubt now in the firmness of "B" Company's belief that all the Fritz's in Germany could not shift them. In no case had the enemy reached closer than 300 yards of the outpost, and, excepting for the still, grey figures dotted all over the landscape, and an odd runner going for his life, with half-a-dozen Aussies having pot shots at him, the scene was as quiet as before the attack.

An "Even Go."

On the left of the 44th, the Bosch had received the same reception, and in no case had he entered an Australian trench. Considering the long frontage and the few men, comparatively speaking, holding it, and the fact that there was practically no artillery support for either side, it was an Australian triumph in what was virtually an "even go" between the Australian and German infantrymen. Even, because if the Aussies were dug in, the Bosche had such an overwhelming superiority in numbers, that if his men could have kept advancing regardless of loss, they must have swamped the few occupants holding the shallow trenches.

The Right Flank.

On the south bank of the Somme, the trenches on "B" Company's right flank were held by some British troops—exhausted remnants of the 5th Army. These trenches were taken by Fritz, and the result was that "B" Company's flank was exposed to machine gun fire from these trenches and Bouzencourt, a collection of houses across the river.

On the night of the 30th, acting under orders, two posts were dug 300 yards in front of the old trenches on the hill. This certainly did not improve the Australian position, but the orders to dig and occupy them were quite positive. On the night of the 31st, "B" Company was relieved by "A" Company, and withdrew to Whizbang Gully, near Sailly-le-Sec, to have a much-needed rest. Their casualties in this affair, out of 180 men, were only four men killed and six wounded—very few, considering the damage they had inflicted on the enemy and the formidable nature of the attack they had repulsed.

"Tony" Howard.

Corp. Tony Howard was one whose death created a gap which was never filled. Right from the inception of the Battalion Tony had been one of those wild and generous spirits, ready to venture life itself on an even throw of the dice, who sacrificed everything on the altar of comradeship.

CHAPTER XIV.

"THE BATTLE OF CORBIE!"

In giving this short sketch of an episode which happened to one company in the Battalion, the writer does so conscious of the fact that the story will be getting criticism from three sources. Firstly, from the members of the other three companies to the effect that "B" Company was not the only unit engaged in winning the war and that probably while "B" Coy. was fighting the "Battle of Corbie," each of the other three was engaged in a similar "strenuous operation" elsewhere, and therefore their tales should be worth the telling also. The answer is that the four companies on the night 27-28 March were so widely scattered that each knew nothing whatever of the other's doings. For that reason, the 44th members who read this story will understand why only the "Battle of Corbie" is chronicled and not the "Battle of Bonnay" or the "battles" named after the places where the other companies were located that night. Secondly, from some of the members of "B" Company, as being an episode that could well be left untold. The answer to that is that it definitely happened, and the incidents of that night have often since been the subjects of interesting reminiscences, and therefore should be recorded. Thirdly, from members of the general public who are interested in reading of the A.I.F. and its doings. Well, the second reason applies to this also. No one claims that the A.I.F. was made up of angels. They were men, with all a man's virtues and vices. In addition, it must be pointed out that for some days prior to the "Battle of Corbie" conditions had been very bad, with continuous travelling by train, 'bus and "per boot," and if any man succumbed to the sudden and unexpected temptation of having unlimited supplies of intoxicating liquors thrust under his very nose, can any civilian, not understanding all the conditions pertaining at the time, blame him? There was one individual responsible—the officer in command of the company—and for his unit's misdeeds that night he blamed himself alone. The military lesson he learnt on that occasion was to the effect that if ordered again to defend a town hurriedly evacuated by its civilian population he would, after making certain that it had not been occupied by the enemy, move his company through the town at the double and only halt them when well out in the open fields on the opposite side, and in addition to the ordinary precautions to be taken in regard to the protection of his front and flanks, he would have to provide effectively for the menace in his rear.

● ● ● ● ● ●

To the Last Man.

No "B" Company man was dinkum unless he served in the "Battle of Corbie." It was the greatest battle of the war, and will live long in history—that is "B" Company history. "B" Company was typically Aussie—composed of hard workers, bad swearers, and good soldiers. They could be led easily, but the officer who tried to drive them died of exhaustion. The company arrived on the Somme at Heilly on March 27th, and at 6 o'clock in the evening, the O.C. told them what they had to do to stop Fritz's steam roller. It was to the effect that the company must proceed to Corbie to defend the bridges across the Somme to the last man!

THE GAP IN THE WIRE!

In nearly all wiring systems which protected trenches **there** were a few gaps. These were left for the con**venience** of the defenders, patrols, etc., and also in **order** to entice the attackers along a definite track which **would** be well protected by machine guns. This shows **a** diagonal gap through Fritz wire. The trench beyond **was** taken, of course, but at the usual cost.

THE LAST 60 DAYS.

In the last sixty days of its existence the Australian Corps was fought almost to a standstill. In the daily "hop-overs," the objectives were always taken, and when taken, the Diggers, with a few sentries to watch their front, would sit down and spell while awaiting the orders for the advance.

"B" Company looked dubious, and the O.C. explained that the Brigadier had specially selected "B" Company out of the whole Brigade for the job, because he knew how they revelled in the "rough stuff." "B" Company put its chest out, and decided that anyhow when they were the last man, they'd detail themselves as the runner back to Headquarters reporting the situation. From there "they" might be sent back as the nucleus, or perhaps get a canteen or some other cushy job.

There was no information available as to the exact whereabouts of Fritz. It was not thought that he had reached Corbie yet, but still, it was possible, and if so he had to be pushed out. Corbie was on the junction of the Ancre and Somme rivers, and was a town of considerable importance from a military point of view. The company moved by platoons at a distance of 100 yards, with No. 7 under Jimmy Everett as an advance guard. Corbie was about six miles from Heilly, and its outskirts were reached at about 9.30 p.m. After patrols had reported "all clear," the company marched in and halted with the leading platoon about fifty yards from the main bridge over the Somme.

The Remnants of the 5th Army "Hanging On."

The occupants of Corbie were about twenty Tommies under a sergeant. They were on guard over the bridge, and the two sentries on duty were doing their tour regimentally, spoiled a bit by the fact that they were plain drunk. There was also two English Engineer officers who had just completed arrangements for blowing up the bridges.

After a consultation with these officers, the two senior officers of "B" Company reconnoitred Corbie and its outskirts around Fouilloy in order to make the best possible dispositions for its defence. They were away from the company for about two hours, and coming back they met the Engineer officers, who walked along to the bridge with them. At the bridge the party was halted and the O.C. nearly bayonetted by the drunken sentry. The sergeant rushed out, incapable of anything but a little speech. For five minutes the O.C. let himself go at this luckless sergeant. His language was inspired, and he ended the outburst by blaming the sergeant for the disaster which had happened to the 5th Army! As the party moved on across the bridge, he told the Engineer officers that it was a disgraceful thing for any man to think of drink at a critical time like this, and that it was the very last thing "B" Company would think of at this stage of the game.

" 'B' Company Would Not Touch It."

A few yards further and a maudlin voice was heard singing "Australia Will Be There!" Then the company-sergeant-major hove in sight, steered by the orderly-room corporal, who was endeavoring to keep him on an even keel. Seeing the O.C., the C.S.M. saluted twice. The O.C. volunteered the information that he was drunk, but the C.S.M. indignantly denied it, and said he hadn't had time yet, as he'd been too busy trying to keep everyone else sober. With instructions to the corporal to find a bed and keep him in it until morning, the O.C. hurried on. No. 7 platoon had been sent in the earlier stages of the evening to patrol the south bank of the Somme, and the roads and approaches beyond Fouilloy, and they were therefore in one sense out of the danger zone, the platoon halted nearest the bridge, being No. 8. As bad luck would have it, in the darkness they had halted right opposite a brewery, and it had not been

THE BATTLE OF CORBIE. 137

long before they had appreciated the situation. They occupied the brewery, and did their level best to prevent any of its contents being captured by the Hun. The platoon commander did his best to stop them, but as fast as he would pull one man out, so another jostled back again, and they made a proper welter of it.

"Hic!"

It was useless wasting words, so the O.C. hurried to the other two platoons. They had not been so lucky as to be halted outside breweries, but still, every second house was an estaminet, so they had not done badly. They were just at the stage when they were ready to fight the whole German Army and call it an even go. Hurriedly, therefore, Mick Anketell's platoon (No. 6) was sent to dig and occupy a trench in a flank position, which covered two of the bridges, and to No. 5 platoon was given the job of patrolling along the north bank of the river. With No. 8 the only thing possible was done, and they were detailed as company reserve at headquarters near the bridge. Precautions were also taken to prevent any further drinking.

When morning dawned Corbie was seen for the first time in daylight. It was an important commercial town (the said commerce being mostly beer), with many imposing buildings, a fine cathedral, and winding paved streets. The shops were well stocked with goods, and were just as the owners had left them only two days before. In the butchers' shops the meat was hanging on the hooks. Bread shops, jewellers, boot shops, and drapers' shops, and last, but certainly not least, estaminets and breweries. Corbie was full of the latter two, and "B" Company could hardly be blamed if the temptation proved too strong.

No. 8 platoon was now staggering to its collective feet, and if ever there was a ragtime platoon it was No. 8 at this stage. However, all four platoons now had a good feed, meat from the butchers' shops and ware in the deserted kitchens soon causing a delicious odour to permeate Corbie's atmosphere.

What Did the O.C. Say?

During the morning a company of 35th Battalion arrived, with orders to take over the defence of Corbie and relieve "B" Company, who were to march back to Bonnay and there await orders. The platoons were pushed out as fast as possible, and ordered to halt in a sunken road about 500 yards from the town. There the O.C. addressed them. What he said does not matter now, but it resulted in dozens of bottles being voluntarily thrown away, "water" bottles emptied, and fervent resolutions by "B" Company that when they next met Fritz they'd make HIM pay for what the O.C. said. They marched to Bonnay with tongues parched, and only water, pure water, to quench their raging thirst, after probably the greatest "bender" in the history of the company!

"The Finest Company in the A.I.F."

How they marched that night to Sailly Laurette, and two days' later broke the Hun attack from that village by their determined defence, has already been told. On the day following that defence and just before relief, the O.C. was wounded, and while being carried off sent the boys a message to say that as far as he was concerned they had well and truly atoned for misdeeds—that he hadn't meant ALL he said when he told them what he thought of them—and that, anyhow, they were the finest company in the A.I.F.!

CHAPTER XV.

"DOB." (LIEUT. R. A. DOBSON).

"Dob" was a reinforcement second-lieutenant who joined the Battalion at St. Pierre after the Paschendale fighting. He was about 40 years of age, and was a well-known figure in Perth business circles prior to enlistment. Receiving his commission, after the usual spell in camps—including six months on Salisbury Plain—he reached the Battalion about the end of October, 1917.

"Dob" was stout, good-tempered and energetic. He reported to the O.C. "A" Company very late on the night when he joined the Battalion, and was told that he would be in charge of No. 3 platoon. He wanted straight-away to have a look at them, and only put it off when informed that he would probably interrupt the poker school.

No. 3 platoon at that time consisted of one sergeant and one man. The remainder were in hospital or had been left on Paschendale's bloody fields. The company next morning fell in on the road (as the least muddy place for a parade ground) in line. The platoon sergeants called the rolls and reported to the C.S.M. He called the company up and reported to the O.C. The O.C. stood the company at ease and told the officers to take post. With a company in line that was two paces in front of the centre of their platoons. "Dob" placed himself two paces in front of his, and when the O.C. ordered platoon commanders to inspect their platoons he turned round, looked his man up and down, sideways, all ways, numbered him, formed him into fours, about-turned him, formed fours again, turned him to his front, and stood him at ease. He then reported his platoon as "All correct!"

The Old Platoon.

"Dob's" platoon was a joke at first, but as reinforcements came along and it filled up, he looked after them like a hen with chickens. He fussed round them, got this for them and that for them, and carried out to the letter the official pamphlet describing the duties of a platoon commander. When the time came to shift to the forward area again, the company of course moved in marching order, platoon commanders carrying packs. At the end of the first day's march, all officers were called to Battalion headquarters and told that the quartermaster had complained that officers' kits were so much over the regulation weight that the transport could not carry them, and that in consequence officers must reduce their kits to the amount allowed, viz., 56lb.

Most of them complied by squeezing their kits tighter and making a smaller volume of the same weight of gear, but "Dob" was dinkum. He was also impressed by what the colonel said, not knowing as much about colonels as the others. He, therefore, reduced his kit to the correct weight, and from the remainder he selected his "British warm" (a very heavy greatcoat) and some other weighty articles, and stuffed them into his already full pack. The remainder he left at his billet, to the tender mercies of the French Madame.

The company marched twenty miles that day, and "Dob" stuck it to the end. They billetted in barns in a French village, and he saw his platoon snug among the straw, and did not stir another yard. The officers were billetted half a mile away, but "Dob," with his boots and coat off, was content to lie among the platoon and rub his feet and get them to rub his back. The next day the "British warm" and other articles went in the transport and "Dob" marched lighter!

"To-morrow, 'Dob.'"

In camp "Dob" was a great organiser of games, and even played with a zest which shamed many a younger man. He had a shower every morning. It was a bitter winter, too, and the Battalion for some time was camped near the Divvy baths. "Dob" would be up at daybreak, have a cold shower, and be back before the noses of his fellow officers showed from under their blankets. They always agreed—after breakfast—that a shower was a fine thing, and that they would start in the morning if "Dob" would wake them. He always tried, but in no case was he more successful than to get a promise to start to-morrow.

"Dob's Diarrhoea Dope."

"Dob" had dreams of big things in commerce after the war. He had an infallible remedy for diarrhoea, which he said would cure the worst case with a couple of doses. After the war he was going to call it "Dob's Diarrhoea Dope," and be a benefactor to mankind. His other scheme was to make himself a millionaire by applying the methods of utilising the waste products of a military camp to every town in Australia. He was to take all the "A" Company officers into this scheme, and float it under the title: "The 'A' Company By-Products Ltd."

However, it was not to be.

"Dob's" first experience in the line was in the Le Bizet sector. He was just the same in the line as out of it—his one thought for his platoon—and, let it be said, they thought there was no officer in the world like "Dob."

The Somme.

When the Battalion was rushed down to the Somme to stem the Hun advance towards Amiens, "Dob" and his platoon were in the thickest of it. He came through safely until he was sent with the nucleus to Bonnay, a village just behind the line. One night in April Fritz shelled this village heavily with gas and H.E., and all troops were ordered out of billets into the open fields. "Dob" got out safely, and then discovered that a Lewis gun had been left in the billet. He and the Lewis gunner went back, recovered the gun, and were just getting out of the village when a shell burst nearby and killed him instantly.

Thus ended the career of "Dob"—one of the finest fellows who ever joined the Battalion.

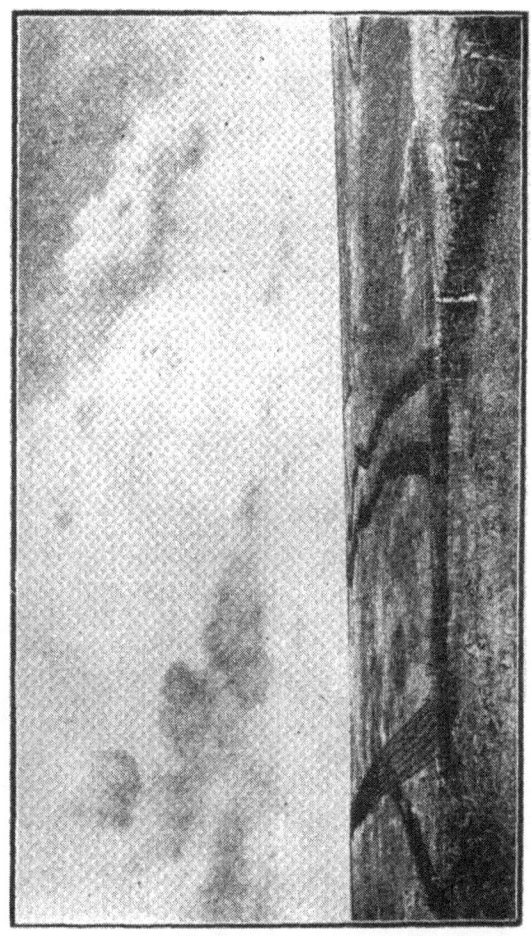

THE WIRE!
The thickness of the wire protecting the Hindenburg Line could hardly be credited. Three belts, each **twenty yards** thick with fifty yards of cleared ground between **each belt.** The whole covered by an extraordinary number of machine guns in concrete emplacements, and fought to the bitter end by their users. It stopped **the** Yanks, but not the Aussies.

THE HINDENBURG LINE.

Fritz put up a stiff fight in his Hindenburg Line, and before he vacated a bay in that tremendous system of trenches he left one or two dead Germans in it, and—too often—one or two dead Aussies.

CHAPTER XVI.

THE ACTION OF HAMEL.

The War of Work!

The whole four companies of the Battalion returned to front line duty the next night (May 1), and remained there for seven days. It was chiefly a matter of work now, and this consisted of digging, wiring and carrying trench necessities to the front line. Then came a period of seven days in support, in which, apart from the incessant working parties, nothing of an important nature occurred. After this the Battalion was given a few days' rest in Heilly. It then took over the front line in the Morlancourt sector, north of Sailly-le-Sec. Here again it seemed that the war had developed into a contest as to which side could work the hardest, and the Diggers' opinion was that the Aussies won easily. However, the whole of this period was a joyful one, comparatively speaking. The artillery on both sides was fairly quiet, and food was more plentiful than it ever had been. Most of the company cookers had cows attached to them, and fresh meat, pork, poultry and eggs were plentiful, although not issued by the quartermaster. The weather was quite decent, and many of the Diggers' quarters, even in the support line, boasted beds and bedding, while a bit further back many of the units had their own pianos.

Villers Brettonneaux.

A move south of the Somme was made towards the end of May, when the front line at Villers Brettonneaux was taken over. Here the usual trench warfare was carried on under conditions much better than those pertaining to the old sectors in Belgium. A feature now was the fact that the trenches, having been dug at the beginning of April, were here enveloped by grain crops. No Man's Land was a field of grain, three feet high, which was full of possibilities for surprises by both sides.

After various tours of duty in the line, in support and in reserve with nothing in particular happening, the Battalion was relieved towards the end of June and marched back to Allonville Wood, there to prepare for its next little "hop over."

Hamel!

The objective on this occasion was to be a line of trenches on the hill beyond the village of Hamel, held by the Hun. Hamel was a small village, situated between Villers Bretonneaux on the south and Sailly-le-Sec on the north. The most complete preparations were made to make the operation a success, the attacking Brigades being the 11th Brigade (left) and the 4th Brigade (right). Tanks were to be extensively used. A new type of tank had been evolved which was very mobile, being able to turn at right angles without any loss of speed. The tank personnel were very keen on making a success of this particular stunt, as they wanted to remove the bad odor in which they were held by the Australians, especially the 4th Division, on account of their failure at Bullecourt.

Introduction to the Yanks.

The 44th met the Yanks for the first time at Allonville Wood; some officers and about one hundred Americans being attached to take part in the Hamel stunt for instructional and experimental purposes. This Yankee business was well muddled. After all

THE ACTION OF HAMEL.

details had been fixed as to the part they were to play, and even after they had commenced the approach march to the assembly area, orders were received the night before the actual attack that they were to be withdrawn. To the credit of the Yanks, a good number heard the order with deaf ears and took part as originally arranged. Some of their officers shed their American uniforms and entered the scrap as Diggers. Many were killed and wounded, and at the action of Hamel the Yank made good.

The trenches which formed the 44th's objective were on a ridge, and were interesting to them in view of the fact that they were the very trenches which the enemy had captured on March 30, and from them enfiladed "B" Company's trenches in front of Sailly-le-Sec.

On the night of July 3-4, the assembly was carried out without a hitch; at dawn the barrage opened and the advance began. At only isolated points was much resistance shown. Pear trench on the 16th Batt. front held up part of their advance, and also the flank of the 44th for a short time, and it was only finally cleared when most of the defenders had been killed, Pte. Axford, of the 16th Battalion, winning his V.C. in the operation.

The Tanks' Wonderful Work.

The tanks did wonderful work. Cruising between the moving barrage and the advancing infantry, they shelled strong posts with their six-pounders, caused havoc with their machine guns, put the "wind" up Fritz, and gave much moral support to the attackers.

The objectives were reached everywhere according to plan. Hundreds of prisoners were captured, and the whole of the German system of trenches was overrun. Consolidation was at once begun, and the necessary praparations made to meet the inevitable counter-attack. At first the Hun artillery was quiet, having been blanketed by the counter-battery fire, used in addition to the moving barrage. During the afternoon, however, it become stronger, and Hamel village (which after capture had been cleared of Australian troops), and the captured trenches were subjected to a very heavy fire.

The Counter-attack!

At about 10 p.m. on the 4th, a counter-attack gained a footing in the 44th line at the junction of "A" and "B" Companies' sectors. This attack was carried out by a small party with bombs up a communication trench leading from the new No Man's Land into the 44th trenches, and it was followed by a larger party of about 200 men who had been hidden in dug-outs in the valley in front of the new line during the day. "A" and "B" Companies had fifteen men captured, most of whom were wounded, and they also lost heavily in killed. This attack caused much local confusion, Fritz becoming well established along about two hundred yards of trench. Arrangements were at once made that "C" Company in support was to retake the line at dawn the next day. Before that organised attack could take place, however, Aussie initiative, audacity, and dash completed the job for them.

The Diggers Run Riot.

Lieut. Dick Cornish, of "B" Company, and Lieut. "Rick" Gaze, M.C., of "D" Company, with fourteen men from various companies, collected all the bombs they could find, hurriedly arranged two bombing parties, and just as dawn broke they went baldheaded at the Huns from both flanks. They drove

THE ACTION OF HAMEL. 149

them from bay to bay in the trench, and finally down the communication trench which they had entered by. In places this was only two feet deep, and there the Bosche got into the open and fled over the top. The two parties followed, flinging bombs, bayoneting, snapshooting, and using the two Lewis guns (one per party) from the hip. Some Germans got away, thirty were killed, many wounded, and one officer and seventy men, together with fifteen machine guns mounted in the trench, were captured. Also eleven out of the fifteen 44th men who had been taken the night before were recaptured. And all this by two officers and fourteen men! It was a wonderful performance, watched by practically the whole of the Battalion, and carried out with a dash that made failure impossible.

When some of the names of the men engaged in this exploit are mentioned, the success of the operation will not be wondered at. In addition to the two officers, the party included Sgt. J. R. Padgett, Pte. Tierney, and Pte. Lynch, all of "C" Company, and Sgt. "Yak" Ingvarsen, of "B" Company. Lynch was absolutely irresistible throughout the whole performance, and it was a thousand pities that this gallant Aussie was killed towards the finish of the little stunt, and at a time when its success was assured. He was shot through the head and killed instantly while in the midst of a crowd of Huns.

German Chivalry.

The experiences of the eleven men re-captured after being taken by Fritz were very interesting. Most of them were wounded and some had already been bandaged by our own stretcher-bearers before they were taken. Although under the existing circumstances small blame could have been attached if the enemy had thought fit to let the 44th wounded wait, his stretcher-bearers bandaged them up, and in the case of Private E. Mercer, who had his thigh shattered, they removed his old bandages and replaced them more carefully and with much professional skill. The only articles they "ratted" the prisoners of were the tinned rations which were always carried in the haversack. The four men not recaptured had been sent back bearing one of his wounded out of the line.

Decorations.

For this very gallant action Lieut. Cornish was recommended for the V.C., but received the D.S.O. instead. Lieut. Gaze was awarded a bar to his Military Cross, and various n.c.o.'s and men who took part received well-earned D.C.M.'s and M.M.'s, among whom were Sgt. Ingvarsen and Pte. Tierney. June 5th and 6th were days of digging under a steady shell fire. The old trenches were very wide and not deep, and the chalk of which the country was composed made the deepening very hard work. On the night of the 6th, the Battalion was relieved, and wended a weary way back to Allonville Wood.

Casualties.

The casualties sustained in this action were 35 killed and 150 wounded and 4 prisoners of war out of a fighting strength of 500. Some good men went West, Charlie Comben and "Doc" Grace, of "B" Company, being two rough diamonds who gained their wooden crosses with honor to themselves and loss and sorrow to their comrades.

CHAPTER XVII.

THE LAST 60 DAYS.

In the Bank at Daours.

The Battalion next moved to Daours, and took up its quarters in a bank just outside the village. The 11th Brigade was in reserve, so that for the next few weeks the Battalion had a quiet time. The numbers were reduced from the thousand that had arrived on the Somme in March to about 600 in July, and many of these had been wounded and rejoined.

It was evident that big things were in the air, but nothing definite was given out. In view of the magnitude of the subsequent battle, the secrecy of its preparation was one of its most notable features. Every opportunity was taken for physical, musketry and Lewis gun training, and with the afternoons devoted to games, swimming and sports and the evenings to concerts, the time passed pleasantly enough, although the lack of civilian companionship was much felt at this time. The swimming parades in the Somme were probably the most enjoyed, as the weather was quite warm and the river formed an ideal bathing place. The greatest drawback at this time was Spanish influenza, which spread right throughout the Battalion and caused many evacuations, and even with those who did not report "sick," the effect could be seen.

On the night of July 31, the Battalion took over the front line near Accroche Wood in front of Hamel— part of the line they had captured on July 4. There was nothing much doing excepting sniping and occasional spasms of artillery. On August 3, tank officers visited the trenches reconnoitreing the front, and this was the first definite information to the troops that a stunt was near at hand. On the next night the Battalion was relieved, and moved back to Hamellette, where instructions were issued that all ranks were to keep to cellars and barns by daylight, and only move about when necessary by night.

The Preparation.

Tanks by the score moved in the hours of darkness into Hamellette, and were camouflaged before morning. Guns in vast numbers moved up and took their allotted positions, and without firing a shot before morning were concealed from the view of hostile aircraft. Huge dumps of stores were created in a single night, and between the hours of dusk and dawn the roads seethed with traffic, all, wonderfully enough, so well organised that not the slightest confusion existed anywhere. By daylight all traffic would cease, and to all appearances there was nothing doing on the Western front except the ordinary business of trench warfare.

Details for the coming stunt were now given out. It was to be the greatest battle of this or any other war. The attacking troops were two Divisions of English troops on the left (north of the Somme), the Australian Corps (five Divisions) in the centre (south of the Somme), and the Canadian Corps (four Divisions) on the right, the whole force being under the command of Lieut.-General Sir John Monash, the Australian Corps Commander, and the objective somewhere near Berlin.

Details were thoroughly worked out. Much use was being made of tanks, and every company of the assaulting infantry was allotted four of them—one to

MACHINE GUN EMPLACEMENT.

This is a concrete machine gun emplacement in the Hindenburg Line. Note the empty cases, which show that before the gunners were put out of action, they had used their weapon extensively.

THE HINDENBURG LINE NEAR BONY.
Note the concrete parapet and firing step, with the typical dug-out entrances. Those dug-outs went down 25 feet, and were joined at the bottom. They were fitted with bunks, tables, and conveniences of all sorts.

work with and co-operate with each of the three platoons of the company, and the other to be used as a reserve. Conferences with the tank officers settled any doubtful questions, and created a feeling of mutual confidence between the two arms.

Assembly.

The Battalion moved to its assembly position on the night of August 7. Everything was quiet, and the approach march was successfully carried out without a casualty. The troops lay in shell holes, and quietly awaited the dawn and the events which lay ahead.

"Germany's Black Day!"

At 4.20 a.m. the barrage came down; at 4.23 a.m. the troops moved forward; at 4.25 a.m. it was not possible to see the hand held at arm's length from the face. The thickness of the fog and smoke blanket that morning was something quite beyond what any Australian had counted on. The whole line became hopelessly mixed, all ranks simply doing the best they could and keeping going somewhere in the direction of their own moving barrage. Company and platoon commanders never even saw their tanks; sometimes they heard them, but that was all. No company or even platoon commander that morning had any influence over his men. He became simply an individual, blind to everything except what he tumbled over, and not knowing anything about the unit he was supposed to be in command of. However, as it happened, there was no need to worry. Every Digger or small party of Diggers when they found themselves apparently isolated pressed on—always in the direction of the barrage. There was no sitting down waiting for orders.

The Advance Goes On.

Passing over the first ridge in the Hun territory, the fog became a little less dense. Isolated parties of Germans were here captured and sent back. Every trench and dugout that was encountered was cleaned up, but the resistance was practically nil. The fog, which at first seemed the undoing of the attack, was the best thing that could have happened, as the Hun never had a target for his machine guns until the infantry were right on top of him.

At 7 o'clock the fog cleared. The troops had now reached the line of their first objective. Every unit was hopelessly mixed, but hasty reorganisation took place, gaps were filled, and digging at once commenced.

The Battery in Malard Wood.

About this time a battery of Fritz artillery came out into the open from Malard Wood, north of the Somme and in front of Chipilly, overlooking the whole of the Australian line. This battery enfiladed the 44th line, and caused many casualties. It also showed that the attack north of the river had failed.

One of the supply tanks at this time was unloading stores in the middle of the 44th line, when one of these shells hit it. Luckily all its crew had come out for a breather, as the concussion started the engine. It went full speed down the hill, and coming to a very steep bank rolled over and over to the road at the foot, where it lay on its back out of action.

The Fourth Divvy!

At 8.20 a.m., "according to plan," the 4th Division came on the scene. Moving in artillery formation, as steady as if on a peace manoeuvre, they passed through the 3rd Division and pushed on "into the blue."

The 4th Division can well be proud of themselves for that day's work. They had marched for miles behind attacking infantry, through thick fog, with direction and touch difficult to maintain, yet they passed through the 3rd Division on time and free from the slightest trace of confusion, looking just as fit and confident as one would expect of any unit with the fighting record of the 4th Australian Division.

The 44th were now able to sit up and take notice. Apart from the shelling from Malard Wood, there was no artillery fire. The British artillery was still shelling the ridges and gullies near Chipilly, and German troops could be seen making disjointed movements in that vicinity. About midday some 4th Divisional artillery engaged in a duel with the battery at Malard Wood, and after a few lively exchanges blew it out of its position and relieved the 44th of a troublesome enemy. During the afternoon, American troops were pushed into action, and they cleared Malard Wood, but only at the cost of very heavy losses.

The 44th now merely occupied their trenches until the night of August 11, when they moved forward to a position in a gully near Morcourt, in rear of the front line established by the 4th Divison.

More Aerial Bombs.

While this move was being carried out in single file across country on a pitch black night, a German aeroplane dropped bombs, one of which practically wiped out "B" Company's headquarters, Lieut. Jim Everett, C.S.M. Quayle, some signallers and stretcher-bearers being very badly wounded.

In the new position, the Battalion remained for two days, digging trenches at night and resting by day. They then moved up to occupy a position in close support to a threatened portion of the line, and after twenty-four hours there moved back on August 14 to old No Man's Land near Accroche Wood.

A Bad-tempered Battalion.

It was an extraordinarily dark night, and there must have been some electrical disturbance in the atmosphere, although it seemed quiet. For some reason all ranks were fed up and bad tempered. Stumbling over the uneven ground caused more outbreaks of language than was usual. There were no jokes cracked, and to cap the lot no one was allowed to smoke on account of the presence of bombing 'planes. It was always usual, if one crowd passed another under these circumstances, to ask and give information as to what unit they each belonged to. Not so on this occasion. It was, "Is that 'D' Company?" "'D' Company what, you ——— fool, do you think there's only one 'D'——— company in this ——— war?" snarled the reply. "'D' Company, umpty umpty," came the return. "Oh! they're where they always ——— are, ——— asleep in a ——— dug-out!" There is no doubt that for some unexplainable reason the Diggers were much less angelic that night than usual.

In old No Man's Land the Battalion bivouaced for a few days. The casualties had been about 20 killed and 70 wounded—very few considering the magnitude of the operation. They then moved across to Chipilly Valley, where they remained for two days, making preparations for their next stunt north of the river.

CHAPTER XVIII.

BRAY.

The front line North of the Somme was now held by the 9th and 10th Brigades, and ran across the plateau west of Bray. An operation was arranged for August 21, in which the 9th and 10th Brigades were to attack, and if successful, the 11th Brigade was to move through them and exploit the success. There was a tremendous artillery barrage covering the attack of these two Brigades, the British artillery being in and on the eastern outskirts of Gressaire Wood.

The Battalion was due to move from Chipilly Gully in the early morning, march through Gressaire Wood, and debouch into the open on the Bray plateau in artillery formation, then move forward for about one thousand yards, dig in, and await the orders to exploit.

The Bray Barrage.

At 8 a.m., as they swung from the wood into the open, they were evidently immediately spotted by enemy balloons, for a tremendous Fritz barrage was placed right across the plateau in front of the advancing troops. This barrage seemed to be a high wall of smoke, dust and flame, and there was not one man looked at it who thought he would ever get through it. However, they tried it—with thick tongues and sticky feelings—with their stomachs in their throats—and only hoping that "theirs" would

be a decent Blighty. There was no excitement, no
buoyancy of spirits in the expectation of meeting
Fritz just on the other side of the barrage; it was just
a plain order that a certain position had to be reached
behind the front line, so as to be ready to do something later. Many men were hit going through. A
shell (all sizes they were, from 8-inch down) would
burst in the middle of a little section, and out of the
smoke and dust would stagger one or two half-blinded
figures. As it cleared perhaps two motionless
figures would be seen, then another with one bending
over him, the last the fortunate survivor, thinking not
of his own marvellous luck, but of his less fortunate
comrade.

When the position to be occupied was reached it
can be understood that the Diggers lost no time in
using their best friends—the pick and shovel—and
a line of posts was dug which ran right across the
plateau astride the Bray-Corbie Road.

The Tommy Artillery.

The 44th took off their tin hats that day to the
Tommy artillery. One battery of six guns was in
the open in front of Gressaire Wood, and while firing
its barrage was spotted by Fritz. He ranged on it—
over—under—and then the range. He concentrated
a number of 8-inch guns on that one battery, and one
by one its guns were put out of action by direct
hits. When engaged in firing a barrage the artillery
had to continue firing as long as a gun was service-
able. Soon only one was left, and it kept spit-
ting away as though the fate of the British Army
rested on its efforts. Several shells came very close,
and then the grand finale, one bursting under the
muzzle, which lifted it over, and killed and wounded
most of the personnel.

The 44th were not, after all, used for exploitation purposes, owing to some hitch on the left flank hanging up the Australian advance. The Battalion's job was simply to sit on that awful plateau with every object on it in full view of the enemy balloons, and take everything he sent over. He was very liberal, too, and he plastered the whole line with every size of shell for the next two days. The Diggers could see no apparent reason for his misplaced energy, but it turned out afterwards that he was preparing to move back and had decided to lighten his load.

The Battalion after this endurance test went back a mile or so, and camped on a hillside along the Somme near Etinghem.

The Luck of the Game.

The night before the move through the barrage six reinforcement officers fresh from Australia joined the Battalion. At 8 o'clock the next morning one of them had collected a piece of shell in the arm, and was off back from whence he came. There were many of the old hands there would have given all they had in the world for half his luck.

"O.C.'s will Ride Horses!"

At the conference when details of the operation were arranged an order was given that officers commanding companies would ride their horses. This caused consternation, as heavy shelling was expected, and a horse under shell fire is a difficult proposition. After discussion it was decided that they could use their own discretion. Needless to say, the horses were left behind—luckily as it happened, because no horse would have ever faced the barrage through which all had to travel that day.

The Attack on Bray.

On the night of August 24 a move forward was made to assemble for an advance beyond Bray at dawn the next day. The assembly was completed, the barrage came down, and the troops moved forward, but not a German was met with until the high ground east of Bray had been occupied, where a number of prisoners were taken. Long-range artillery and gas shelling were the only enemy measures employed here to delay the advance.

The Daylight Patrol.

On the slope beyond Bray was Ceylon Wood. The outpost line at the finish of the advance had the wood just in front of it, and Capt. M. Lewis, M.C., Lieut. O'Carroll, M.M., and Sgt. Gillett went forward and patrolled it in broad daylight. By a lot of bluff and a little knowledge of the German language possessed by Captain Lewis, they persuaded 35 Germans to surrender, after the Germans had got in first on the draw and covered them with their rifles.

Not Yet for the Aussies.

Before this Bray operation took place, the Diggers were informed that it would be the end of stunting for the year. All they had to do was to capture that high ground east of Bray, and it was to be the Aussies' line, to simply hang onto and make comfortable until the next spring campaign. Well, it was taken, but as for the sitting tight part of the business, it was not yet for the Aussies.

CORBIE CHURCH.

The author feelingly directs the attention of members of "B" Company to the sign on the left building (Beer, Wine, Champagne, Wholesale).

"SOMME" POULTRY.

The Brass Hat: "Hu-r-r-r, my man! What the devil are you doing with that fowl?"

Digger: "Well, sir, to tell you the truth, it's like this: When the people left these farms they didn't take their fowls with 'em, and they got very wild. And when I was coming along the road this one rushed out at me and tried to bite me, and I had to kill it in self-defence, after a hard struggle, and I'm now taking it along to show my O.C., so that he'll understand why I'm late for parade."—(C. M. Gould, in "Aussie.")

CHAPTER XIX.

THE ADVANCE ALONG THE SOMME.

Daily "Hop-overs."

Fritz was evidently feeling the effects of the August battles, and the powers that be wisely decided to push on. Therefore, for the next fortnight the Brigade advanced, took a position, consolidated, and advanced again. The Battalions of the Brigade took turn and turn about at firing line and support, and shared whatever was going equally between them. There were a few casualties every day from machine gun, rifle and shell fire, because, except at Bray, Fritz never vacated any position voluntarily, and had to be pushed back every yard that he retired.

On one occasion, near Suzanne on August 26, the 44th "hopped the bags" three times in the twenty-four hours. Casualties were suffered, but the objective was taken on each occasion. By the end of August, therefore, it can be realised that all ranks were feeling the effects of the strenuous part they had played since August 8. The strength of the Battalion had been reduced by battle casualties, until at this period it mustered only two hundred and fifty almost physically exhausted fighting men.

"Three Weeks—Perhaps!"

Marching, fighting and digging along the Somme, through Curlu and Hem to Clery-sur-Somme, was a continuous nightmare, with most of the chief events becoming only a blur on the memory, and the outstanding feature to every individual being his own physical fatigue. On one occasion "D" Company was detached to advance as a liaison company with the Tommies on the left flank, and although only with them for 24 hours they collected eighty-one prisoners (half as many again as their own strength) as their share of this little stunt.

On September 3 the Battalion was relieved, and ordered to a quarry near Hem for a spell. The Diggers, on Divisional authority, were definitely informed that the rest would be for ten days at least, three weeks perhaps, and possibly one month. All hands worked hard and cheerfully that day making comfortable homes for themselves, digging their sleeping quarters in the sides of the quarry, building headquarters and cook-houses, and a very tired Battalion retired that night to blissfully dream of the long spell in store.

"Move at Dawn."

At midnight orders came from Brigade that the Battalion was to be ready to move at dawn. A hurried conference of officers decided to take a risk with the Brigadier rather than with the men, and not disturb them until morning, in the hope that the move would come off later in the day. As it happened it was 9 o'clock when the Battalion had to move, and the opinions of the Diggers on the war, the Bosch, staff officers and everything in general were unprintable! A march along roads crammed with transport, and that night the 44th bivouaced on the famous Mont St. Quentin, which had fallen to the Fifth and Sixth Brigades the day before. Those Brigades must have put up a wonderful performance, considering that the position was impregnable from a military point of view, and that the Battalions taking part must have had the rough time during the preceding month that every Australian Battalion had. They had lost

ADVANCE ALONG THE SOMME.

many men in the operation, but for every dead Aussie lying on the Mont when the 44th occupied it there must have been twenty Germans who had fought it out to the bitter end.

At dawn on September 5 the 44th pushed on through Peronne to Doingt as the advanced troops. Resistance became slight, and the advance went on so rapidly that it was mainly a question as to how far the physical condition of the troops would take them each day, the keeping of touch with flank and rear and the transmission of information as to the exact whereabouts of the front line troops.

Fritz now was going back as fast as he could. He was fighting a stubborn rear-guard action with machine guns and artillery; but even so, his main body was unduly hurried and harried by the rapidity, determination, and persistency of the Australian advance. All descriptions of guns and transport, stores and dumps were captured, and for miles in rear of his line dumps and villages were burning and being blown up. They were thrilling moments, these!

The frontage of each Battalion at this stage was about 2500 yards—a wide front considering that the strength of most Battalions was in the neighborhood of two hundred and fifty men. However, it was sufficient.

Those Van-guard Stunts.

A feature about this time was the fact that vanguards were formed under the senior C/O Battalion. In the case of the 44th, Lieut.-Col. Clark became O/C van-guard, consisting of 44th and 41st Battalions of Infantry, one squadron Australian Light Horse, some Engineers and A.M.C., and two Brigades of Artillery. It was quite a good scheme, but rough on the Battalion staff of the O/C van-guard, which in addition to looking after its own Battalion, had to write and transmit orders and information to each one of the units of which the van-guard was composed.

The old Battalion carried on through Buire, Tincourt and Cartigny until Roisel and Bernes were reached, the latter being two villages not far from the outposts of the famous Hindenburg Line. At the end of the last day of this advance, about the middle of September, all hands were so tired that, reaching the sunken road which marked the limit of the advance for the day, they simply lay down and slept without any attempt at digging the customary holes in the bank as protection from artillery. That night they were relieved as van-guard, and after two days in a wood near Buire, they marched back to Doingt, a village near Peronne, there to have a fortnight's dinkum spell after six weeks of strenuous activity and crowded incident.

TO HEADQUARTERS of 44th Batt. A.I.F.

No. CR 15 Date 8·8·18 PIGEON SERVICE.

"A" Coy. 44th Batt. is digging in on GREEN LINE from Q14c41 to Q14a62 aaa. Units are mixed very much aaa Will reorganise after digging in aaa Am in touch with 35th Batt on right and 'C' Coy. 44th Batt. on left aaa. No enemy artillery aaa. Our own is firing short and some are falling behind and on line aaa Everything on this front seems clear for 4th Div. to go through. aaa

FROM Longmore Capt.
p.n. o/c 'A' Coy. 44th Bat
TIME 8 a.m.
PLACE Green line

No. of copies sent by PIGEON SERVICE.
Please stop artillery getting on line CR

TIME of RECEIPT at LOFT.

A PIGEON MESSAGE SENT IN ACTION.

On account of the fog and consequent confusion on August 8, runners had a very difficult job in finding those to whom their messages were addressed. Each company carried pigeons, and this is one of the messages sent by feathered means that day. Just as the message was being signed, one of our own shells mentioned (they were 6-inch too) burst right on the parapet of the shallow trench in which a section was digging, killing one man and wounding some others—hence the postscript, although it was almost certain that nothing could be done, and that the short shooting must be borne for another 20 minutes, when it was timed to lift as the 4th Division went through. For the benefit of readers not ex-A.I.F., the Q14c41, etc., denotes the exact position on the map where the company was digging. The letters A.A.A. are the military method of denoting a full stop. The Green Line was the objective of the 3rd Division that day.

CHAPTER XX.

COMMUNICATIONS.

The wonderful advance made by the Australian Corps since August 8 had been made possible only by the remarkably efficient methods of communication right throughout the Corps. The five Australian Divisions, with their artillery, transport and impedimenta, had advanced from August 8 to September 15 a distance of thirty miles, in the face of a more or less determined resistance by a skilful enemy.

Orders from Corps to Division, to Brigade, to Battalion, to Company, to Platoon, and to the individual soldier, were transmitted with clearness and rapidity, and they were based on the information sent back from the front line in the same rapid manner. This efficiency in rapid communication of orders and information alone made it possible to carry out the remarkably bold operations which General Monash performed with the Australian Corps.

With the Battalions the methods used were runners, field telephones and telegraphs generally, with pigeons as an auxiliary. Touch with the flanks was obtained by each unit detailing an officer or n.c.o. to act with its flank unit, with instructions to report progress and events at certain hours or whenever necessary.

The German field telephone wire was very thin, not being insulated like that of the British, and therefore much more could be carried by one man. During the Somme advance the 44th signallers salved this German wire, and by using it were able to get telephonic communication from the front line to Battalion headquarters, within an hour or so after the front line and the new headquarters had become established.

It was remarkable how often these wires became broken by shell bursts. In every such case linesmen would go out, night or day, from each end of the line and examine it until the break was discovered, and communication resumed.

The Runners.

Australian runners reached an extraordinary standard of efficiency. If a message was handed to a runner on a dark night with instructions to deliver it to a certain unit, "exact whereabouts unknown, but possibly at so-and-so," it was certain, if that unit was within miles of the indicated spot, that the message would be delivered. In the darkness, among the outposts, amid mud and wire, memory does not register a runner ever returning with a message undelivered. A truly marvellous record.

The Sigs.

The same with the signallers. If by any improvisation they could establish necessary communication between two points, it was done. With flags, lamps or telephone, if one way was impossible the "Sigs.'" ingenuity could be depended upon to find some other method of "carrying on."

Lieut. Eric McKenzie was in charge of the signallers during the Somme advance, and backed up as he was by a body of men who had had their peace training clinched by much actual service experience, and with every one of them a specialist and an enthusiast, the result was that the Battalion communications were efficient to the smallest detail, and this meant that every operation could be ordered by the C/O knowing full well that in this most essential part of modern war he could absolutely rely on the human machinery at his disposal.

CHAPTER XXI.

THE 44th's FINAL FIGHT.

Bony (The Hindenburg Line).

The 44th camped in huts at Doingt for about a fortnight. The idea was to rest the troops as much as possible, and this of course was appreciated by the Diggers. The fighting strength was now only 220 men. What a difference compared with the first engagement on the Somme in March! However, numbers did not count in the fighting efficiency of any Australian Battalion. Esprit de Corps had reached a standard where every Digger reckoned that his own particular Battalion was more than a match for anything fighting in the Great War. Also, the Diggers, who, as critics of generals and stunts, knew what they were talking about, had formed the general opinion at this stage that, although they had had the last ounce taken out of them in their big advance, they had been well directed, and their generals, especially the Corps Commander, General Sir John Monash, knew their jobs.

The Mutiny.

On account of the shortage in numbers and the fact that the British Army organisation had reduced the number of Battalions in a Brigade to three, an attempt was made to disband the 42nd Battalion and divide its members among the other Battalions in the 11th Brigade. Like Battalions in other Divisions, the 42nd Diggers refused to be disbanded, their argument being that as the 42nd Battalion they came into the war and as the 42nd they'd go out of it. Even-

"APRES LA GUERRE."

"Monsieur," "Madame," "Marie," and le Petit Garcon" Dream of Other Days.
—Drawn by C. H. Percival, in "Aussie."

A tank hauling a disabled "cobber across a trestle bridge after the August 8 stunt.

THE 44th's FINAL FIGHT.

tually, as the time was coming for another stunt, instructions wisely came through that "owing to the imminence of battle, units would not be disbanded." This made the mutiny shortlived.

The 1st and 4th Divisions, while the other three were resting, had attacked and captured the outposts of the famous Hindenburg Line. They had handed their gains over to fresh American Divisions and were then withdrawn from the line altogether.

The Last "Hop-over."

The 44th now prepared for what was to be its last fight. This was the attack on the tremendous Hindenburg system, with two full-strength American Divisions to break it, and the 3rd and 5th Australians advancing behind them with the job of exploiting the Americans' success.

The Yanks Sit Down.

The Yanks went over the top on the morning of September 29. Fog, smoke and lack of experience, however, made their attack a failure—complete on the left in front of the 3rd Division and partial on the right in front of the 5th Division. Some of them got through and pushed on "into the blue." Others sat down when they met resistance and waited for the fog to clear and something to happen. Those who pushed on did not mop up dug-outs, and Fritz came out behind them and manned his machine guns with deadly effect on the Yanks.

The Belts of Wire.

When the 44th, moving in artillery formation, reached the wire in front of the Hindenburg Line, they found it held by Fritz, and instead of a steady march over all that ground, they had to fight bitterly every inch of their way. They overcame these tremendous obstacles—fought the enemy machine gunners, and drove them from their guns. They broke through the wire—and that wire was in three belts, each twenty yards thick, with about fifty yards of cleared ground between each belt—and then they pushed on past the Hindenburg Line. "A" and "B" Companies finally found themselves on the Canal Tunnel between Bellicourt on the right and Bony on the left. The attack on the right had prospered more than on the left, so that "C" and "D" Companies were further back, but in the Hindenburg Line itself.

A Defensive Flank to the 5th Division.

The enemy on the left now came out of the Canal Tunnel in swarms and reinforced the Hindenburg Line near Bony. On the ridge in front of "A" and "B" Companies at this stage was a battery of artillery which shelled them over the open sights with unmerciful accuracy. A hurried consultation by the officers on the spot was held, and as a result a communication trench was occupied leading from the Canal Tunnel to the Hindenburg Line (reference map Wiancourt A27b). Here touch was established with "C" and "D" Companies, who had had an equally hard fight to get their position. Their resistance had been mostly in the shape of machine guns, and their numbers had been sadly reduced before they got into their present location. Touch was now established with a Battalion of the 5th Division on the right and the 43rd Battalion on the left. The latter were astride No Man's Land, and the rest of the 3rd Division were hung up practically in the front line, from which the Americans had attempted their disastrous attack that morning.

The 44th now found themselves astride the Hindenburg system, forming a flank which protected the 5th Division on the right. Fritz made many attempts to break this flank defence, trying in the

THE 44th's FINAL FIGHT.

morning over the top, when machine gun and rifle fire shattered them, and also along the Hindenburg Line with bombs.

The Americans Demoralised.

The Americans, of whom there were hundreds about, were utterly demoralised and disorganised. They had lost every atom of cohesion, and Australian officers were instructed wherever possible to augment their own depleted platoons by attaching Americans to them.

Bony—the Key Position.

The stunt by the afternoon of the 29th was acknowledged a failure. The only thing to do was to hang on to the ground already gained and by small local attacks improve the position wherever possible. The 44th were much troubled by machine guns and "minnies" from Bony, where the Hindenburg trenches dominated the whole line. Fritz had machine guns so placed there that he could plough up in places the bottom of the trenches occupied by the 44th. The only way out was to take Bony. Over the top was out of the question, as the enemy had every advantage in numbers and position, so that bombing attacks were commenced along the Hindenburg Line (which consisted of two trenches, front and support, with C.T.'s every hundred yards). Fritz fought with more dash and vim against the 44th in their last fight than he'd ever produced before.

Nevertheless, the bombing parties pushed on. They had to fight for every bay gained and for the thousand yards of trenches which were gained in this way, the enemy left a dead Hun in every bay. At one bombing block where he put up an exceptional fight, there were seven dead Germans when the 44th took it.

Fritz fought with desperation and determination, and it was not until the next afternoon (September 30) that Bony was taken. This meant that the enemy's last chance of turning the check into a decisive defeat had passed away.

Relieved.

On October 1 the Battalion was relieved from the firing line, and moved back a few hundred yards. The next day they moved up again and occupied the trenches near Bony, which was now slightly in rear of the front line. On the night of October 3, 1918, they were relieved by fresh English troops, and what was left of the 44th moved out of the Big Fight for the last time, and assembled in a quarry west of Hargicourt.

The old Battalion had done exceptionally well in its last stunt. It was the only Battalion in the 3rd Division to get through the Hindenburg Line on September 29, and it got through at a place where the Americans failed.

"But 80 Marched Out!"

By holding the communication trench and the Hindenburg Line itself on the left flank of the 5th Division, the Battalion undoubtedly saved that Division from a very ugly situation. Of the two hundred and twenty fighting men who advanced into that last fight, but eighty marched out—less than half the number of a decent-sized company. The artillery fire over the open sights on the first day was responsible for most of "A" and "B" Companies' losses, while "C" and "D" got theirs principally from machine gun fire in front of the Hindenburg Line, and they also lost heavily in the bombing attacks along it.

Individuals.

Sergeant J. E. V. K. ("Yak") Ingvarsen, D.C.M., of "B" Company, was recommended for the Victoria Cross on account of his dash on the first day. He rushed a machine gun which was holding up a company of Americans, killed the gunner, and chased the remainder of the crew along the trench, running along the parapet and snapshooting at the Huns below. However, the 44th, as was the case with their three previous recommendations for the fighting man's greatest honor, had no luck again, and all the "Yak" received was a bar to his D.C.M.

Sergeant J. R. Padgett, of "C" Company, was awarded the American Distinguished Service Cross for gallantry on the first morning. In addition to flinging Fritz's own bombs back before they had time to explode, he went out into the open and brought in under heavy fire an American soldier, who had been badly wounded. "A," "C" and "D" Companies lost their commanders on the first day. Capt. Morrie Lewis, M.C., commanding "B" Company, was slightly wounded, but "carried on." After Capt. Bremner, M.C., had been wounded, Lieut. E. McKenzie took command of "D" Company, and had the unusual honor after the stunt of being recommended for the Military Cross (which was eventually awarded him) by his own n.c.o.'s, who stressed his gallantry in the bombing attacks towards Bony. When Capt. Hunt was hit, the command of "A" Company once more fell to Lieut. R. Maddeford, M.C. This made the fourth occasion on which the command of "A" Company had fallen to the latter officer in stunts in which its "permanent" commander had been killed or wounded. Capt. "Dickie" Fowler, the "petite" commander of

K

"C" Company, received his issue from a machine gun in front of the wire, where Lieut. McDermott, a newly promoted officer in the same company, was killed.

A Fitting Climax.

It was a fitting climax to the fighting career of the Battalion. They had been in action for nearly two years, had lost in battle four hundred and thirty-three all ranks killed, and one thousand three hundred and forty-six wounded. Had never lost a trench. On only one occasion had they failed to do exactly what they set out to do (that was the 13th March raid). Had captured hundreds of German prisoners, yet in the whole two years had lost only eight prisoners to the enemy!

The Battalion on October 5 was moved back to a village near Amiens. They were now among civilians for the first time since March, after six months in the war-shattered areas, which had created a longing for civilian companionship.

The Armistice.

There they rested. Sick and wounded rejoined and rebuilt the companies.

Then on November 11 came the Armistice, and the war was over—to the indescribable relief of the fighting men.

CHAPTER XXII. (Conclusion).

LOOKING BACK.

Looking back on the part played by the Australian Corps on the Somme from August 8 to October 5, 1918, a period of sixty days, it is safe to say that never has a more strenuous or successful campaign been fought in history. In spite of anything written to the contrary, the Hun was a brave and skilful fighter, and there was never a mistake made by his opponents that he did not take full military advantage of. Although at the time it seemed that too much was being asked of the troops, the results proved that the Corps Commander's judgment was correct, and that it was better to keep tired troops pushing even to the extent of the last ounce of their physical powers, than to allow an equally tired enemy the opportunity of reorganising his forces and defences.

Certain it is that the fighting troops were always backed up by a wonderfully efficient organisation directing their movements in front and supporting them from behind—supply, transport, and the hundred and one other details pertaining to an Army in the field worked just as smoothly and effectively as though the front was stationary.

Demobilisation.

During the waiting period prior to embarkation for Australia, time was passed by educational and sporting stunts. Leave was freely given and opportunities were made for all ranks to obtain civilian employment in England. Even so, time hung heavily, and a man's only feeling was joy when warned for Aussie by a certain draft. Gradually the units were reduced, and finally, in the early part of 1919, the 44th Battalion A.I.F. ceased to exist.

While memory lives, however, the Fighting Forty-Fourth will never die. To be with them Over There was a privilege and an honor —a glorious page in any man's life. And when the Final Evening comes to us all, and the Last Pipe has been smoked, it will be of the comrades who wore the blue and white oval patch that we'll be proudly thinking. Theirs was a tradition that Australia will do well to perpetuate while there's a growing generation of free men left to be inspired by it.

DEAR OLD "BLIGHTY."

A Tribute to Her Pluck and Hospitality.

The wonderful part the civilians of the British Isles played in the Great War will never be forgotten by the Diggers, and it is certain that if the Australian public generally only realised the extent to which the English people went in order to show their appreciation of the part played by the Dominions, then the bond of Empire would be even more securely cemented than it is to-day.

Every Digger in England on convalescence was given the opportunity of being a guest in some English home, where the best was not good enough for him, and his hosts went to no end of trouble and expense to make his stay an enjoyable one. Of course, the Digger, with his unconventional ways, soon made himself at home, and made the task of catering for his amusement an easy one. The Digger in hospital was made a special charge of by the English women, and on visiting days they thronged through the wards, giving words of cheer to lonely Diggers and always leaving packets of "fags" or some other welcome luxury for his use. The general feeling, too, in England was a marvellous one, considering that most of the manhood of the nation was engaged overseas and the daily casualty lists from all fronts of their own folk were tremendous. Yet the optimism and cheerfulness which met the war-weary Digger in England on leave after a morale-wracking stunt made a new man of him, and caused him to return to his unit inspired.

Quite apart from the nation's military and naval efforts, which astounded the world, the never-say-die spirit exhibited by the English civilian in times of food shortage and defeat in battle brought to mind vividly that there was much truth in the old, old saying: "Blood will tell."

For the rest of their lives the Aussies will remember the people of dear old Blighty with a gratitude that comes right from the heart.

THE FRENCH AT HOME.

An Appreciation of a Wonderful People.

The verses called "A Heroine of Bois Grenier," published recently, prompt these few lines in appreciation of French folk in general. There is no doubt whatever that the impression gained by actual contact was that the national morale of the French people was something for visitors to wonder at, and for the nation to be proud of, which, "apres la guerre," the French soldier could look back on with pride in the thought that, while he was fighting stubbornly in the trenches, his women-folk and the old parents left behind were "carrying on," and creating just as good an impression in their sphere as he was in his, which is saying a mighty lot.

When the Aussies look back and remember the little French farmhouse, with its cheery Madame, and perhaps one or two laughing Mademoiselles; its wonderful stove (and their stoves were wonderful), the simple kitchen with its spotless brick floor—they will perhaps marvel now at the means whereby steak and eggs, coffee and bread, were always forthcoming so readily, and in such generous quantities.

Madame never seemed the least put out even when her kitchen was uncomfortably crowded with hungry Diggers, but how she managed to satisfy them will ever remain a mystery.

And the day when the boys left for the line, with Madame and the girls standing at the door waving handkerchiefs, with tears streaming down their faces. They knew only too well that they were seeing many a "bon Australien" for the last time.

In the villages just behind the line the women of France endured many of the dangers which are commonly supposed to belong only to the fighting men. Shell-fire and gas took a heavy toll of casualties, and the conditions under which they stuck to the ruins of their homes had to be seen to be properly appreciated. Even the little children attended school with tiny gas masks hanging over their shoulders. Their sleeping quarters were in cellars; their amusements were nil; yet almost under trench conditions these wonderful people of France showed smiling faces, and had a cheery word always for their beloved "Australiens." For the stiff upper lip they showed right through the Great War, and the way they kept their farms and homes going in the absence of their men folk, these lines are penned as a tribute to the magnificent national spirit of France.

www.ingramcontent.com/pod-product-compliance
Lightning Source LLC
Chambersburg PA
CBHW031955080426
42735CB00007B/405